LOST
&
FOUND

LOST
Love/companionship/social order

&

FOUND
Pragmatic solutions for life-altering challenges

A WIDOWER'S GUIDE TO SURVIVAL

Written by Robert W. Swanson

Copyright © 2007 by Robert W. Swanson.

Library of Congress Control Number: 2007903387
ISBN: Hardcover   978-1-4257-6297-1
               Softcover   978-1-4257-6296-4

All rights reserved. No part of this book may be reproduced or transmitted in any form or by any means, electronic or mechanical, including photocopying, recording, or by any information storage and retrieval system without permission in writing from the copyright owner.

This book was printed in the United States of America.

To order additional copies of this book, contact:
Xlibris Corporation
1-888-795-4274
www.Xlibris.com
Orders@Xlibris.com
38943

CONTENTS

Preface 9

Beginning of the Beginning 11
Work in Progress 13
Nutritional Challenges 16
To Date or Not to Date? 20
Understanding Contemporary Women 25
Meeting a New Lady 35
Help from Counselors 39
Cloning 43
Online Dating 45
What Would Mother Think? 49
The *M* Word 51
Keeping the Old "Bod" Ticking 53
Dollars and Sense 57
Sell or Stay 60
Keeping House and Hearth Together 63
A Closet of Memories 66
Bills, Bills! 68
Final Tribute 71
Being a Single Grandparent 76
Traveling Single 84
Spirituality 89
How Others See Us 92
End of the Begining 95

Book Endorsements 97

Dedication

This work is created as a memorial to my loving wife, Elizabeth Ann O'Neill Swanson, 1929-2005. A poem written by Fred Wills, father of columnist George Will, expresses well my personal feelings.

The warm sun
Beams through the clear air
Upon glistening leaves.
And the birds
Sweep in long arcs
Over the green grass.
They seem to say,
This might last forever,
But it doesn't.

PREFACE

After the last floral tribute has wilted and well-meaning out-of-town relatives and friends have departed, you will wake up to the *first* day of the rest of your life. Your bed will seem more massive than ever because your mate will never be beside you again. The home you happily shared will be eerily quiet, missing are the comforting sounds of a coffeemaker perking in the kitchen. The jolly, effervescent morning announcer on your alarm radio seems to be terribly out of character. As you adjust your eyes and mind to the new dawn's light, it will slowly become apparent that you are now a *single* man. And with it rolls in an uncomfortable feeling of being very **LOST.**

What happened? Men are *not* the ones to be left behind. Women (God love 'em) from the beginning of time have outlived men, but not in *your* case. You are now (and it is certainly not voluntary) on your own to cope with the future without the love and companionship of your loving mate. Your comfortable social order has all but vanished, and you will be very lonely.

Sociologists often state that ***loneliness*** is a powerful catalyst for extreme mental suffering, often more than any other experience of the human condition. Most men feel they have *lost* life's guiding compass. Hence, the first part of my title is **"LOST."**

This book is *not* intended to be another tome on grieving. Our libraries and bookstores are filled with well-written works on this sensitive subject. However, few works have ever been published containing practical methods to guide new widowers through the life-altering challenges—health, housekeeping, meal preparation, budgets, finances, dating, etc.

This writer was left behind after a blissful marriage of forty-one years. In the following pages, you'll find some steps I have **FOUND** that helped me work though the unexpected. Hence "**FOUND**" is the second part of the book's title. I have lived every inch of what I have written. I sincerely hope what you read will help you comfortably travel the "lost and found" of your forthcoming journey.

Robert W. Swanson
Largo, Florida

THE BEGINNING OF THE BEGINNING

One of the most time-worn clichés is from an ancient Chinese philosopher: "The *first* step is the start of a *lo*ng journey." Dear fellow widowers, we are now taking our *first* steps in a long and often tedious life-altering journey. It is not by choice that we are on this road weighted down with the sad ending of a lovely dream. The path ahead may be littered with uncomfortable challenges reaching the very depths of our souls. At the starting gate, most of us are truly LOST. How well we *individually* proceed is so personal, so unalterably tied to our surroundings, that a book offering the proven path to total "recovery" has yet to be written and probably never will be. When we have FOUND methods that work for us, we then can begin to see the bright lights of a future life. Navigating the way ahead will have many sharp turns and steep hills. But it is the only road to happiness, so let's start our engines.

It is often said that women grieve and men replace. Therefore, one well-traveled way is to *immediately* begin to seek and find a replacement for your departed spouse. To quote John Selby's excellent book *Solitude, The Art of Living with Yourself,*

> A rebound relationship is not a solid relationship, but just an attempt to ease pain by substituting a new person for the one lost. The grafting process might temporally ease the pangs of loneliness, but in the long run it interferes with the healing process. And the new relationship explodes at some point and leaves us in

worse shape than if we had faced our solitary condition honestly and alone.

To add weight to the above, the Census Bureau reports that second marriages are very risky, with a 60 percent failure rate. Little wonder, counselors tell us emphatically to *wait a year or two* before venturing into any serious relationships, more about this in the following pages.

As we go through heartbreak and healing, everyday mundane issues come sharply into focus—making beds, house cleaning, washing dishes, the laundry, paying bills, and picking up medical prescriptions. These tasks continue on without the slightest concern for our mental state of readiness.

Analysts and psychologists can pontificate and probe our souls offering compassionate introspection, but they don't wash our dishes, change our bedding, and prepare our meals. It is to these day-to-day demands that I have tried to offer no-nonsense, serviceable answers.

Some of you readers may be well trained by your dear departed wife in the art of domesticity. Some of you will be in my shoes with little or no training to face an unfamiliar world of home and hearth. I was an experienced, proficient "hunter gatherer" while my lovely wife was an incredible "cave keeper," ensuring our place was neat and tidy while adroitly transforming "raw carcasses" into fantastic feasts. For forty-one years, we each had our set place in a closely defined social order. Now that wondrous order has been turned on end, and responsibilities have been drastically shifted.

In the months that have passed since my wife's death, I have moved from a minor league player to a spot on an AAA roster. I'm ready to open my playbook to any of you seeking to follow this path. Please keep in mind that I'm not ready for the World Series, but I am trying. And with God's help and the support of family and friends, I'll hit a home run, and you can too!

WORK IN PROGRESS

Life is what happens when you are making other plans.
—John Lennon

You probably have already noticed how so many friends and relatives tend to equate divorce or the passing of a close friend, parents, etc. with *your* plight. Let's be very frank about it. The pain from the death of a beloved wife *supercedes* all others. Only those who have gone through the gates of this abyss can truly empathize with *the man left behind*. Fighting the phantom of **loneliness** is the first challenge. Believe me, a feeling of being "lost" will tax your entire being for some time to come!

The above chapter title may seem a bit terse, but let's face reality—as widowers (using a bit of poetic license), we can be properly classified as **works in progress.** Translation? We are now on an uncharted course to *rebuild* our very lives, to find the pathways for future well-being.

Depending on when you pick up this book, your *work in progress* may be well under way. Perhaps you have laid a good foundation and are moving up to start the second floor. For many readers; however, the brick and mortar may not have arrived, and the project may be on hold. It is for these sufferers that I would like to unfold some building plans. There are several routes you can take to begin this massive rebuilding project.

It was not raining when Noah built the ark.
—Howard Ruff

I'm rather sure that after our wives die, the first temptation to approach our new life situation is to just stay in bed and pull the covers over our heads, cut ourselves off from the world, and feel we have been *cheated* out of a happiness few have known. Yes, **cheated**! Some deadly disease or terrible mishap has carried away your lover, best friend, keeper of your home, mother of your children. You certainly didn't ask for this, and *why*, oh, why, did it happen? Was God striking back for our past sins? Hardly!

Each of us entered the unwanted state of *widowerhood* from different paths in life—some rich, some poor; some of us old, some very young; from different races and religions. No matter where we came from—economically, ethnically, or spiritually—the destination we arrived at is tragically the same. For the first time in years, we feel LOST! "LOST"—a word associated with many different images, such as deprived, forsaken, deserted, wretched, abandoned, and confused. Maybe we can sum it up with a simple word—"numb"!

When I say "lost," I don't mean to deprecate the support of our families and close friends; how could we even consider surviving this pain without them? But underneath it all, each of us, as "rookie" widowers, is *a work in progress*. Our devoted loved ones cannot be expected to carry the tools we need to get under way. On the outside, we can force a smile and an air of doing OK, but on the *inside*, we can't help but be worried, more like *afraid* of the future. It's only natural. After all, we have lost half of our being; we feel the *best* half.

That wonderful person who cared for our shirts, kept socks together, tended the garden, wore sexy lingerie, and the beat goes on. All that is now lost.

As we *mentally* recall the memories of a wonderful life with our wives, we are forming a *frozen* vision of *past* happiness. Nothing wrong in reliving the *best of the best*. When one more friend or acquaintance says to me, "Robert, you just have to live *one* day at a time," I will resist the tendency to smack them in their well-meaning faces.

Living *one* day at a time is NOT THE APPROACH! If that was the proven way, the affirmative, then just stay in bed with the covers pulled tight. No, a million times, NO! You are NOT deceased! Pinch yourself to prove it. There's a *new* life to live, and now is the *first* day of it. View the world outside through a new prism and begin to focus on the rest of your life.

Hold it! I'm sounding like a football coach at half-time trying to pep up a losing team; however, what I'm attempting to do with a few words is help you focus on that realization that we, as widowers, are all *works in progress*, and that requires some *long-range* planning. No one-day-at-a-time stuff. Let's all think BIG! Can't you hear the whistle is blowing to start work? Come on "fellow" widowers, get out of that symbolic bed and shower and shave, look in the mirror, and count the blessings you have *right* now!

My late father used to quip, "If you wake up and can stand beside the bed without help and see you are not in jail, it is the start of a good day!" A rather homily philosophy, but it rings true. So where do you turn to find the blueprints for a new life? Again, look in the mirror. It is all there waiting *inside* you.

> *It is better to know some of the questions than all of the answers.*
> —James Thurber

NUTRITIONAL CHALLENGES

If I had my life to live over again, I'd live over a delicatessen.
—author unknown

Keeping body and mind together after the loss of your wife is a monumental nutritional challenge. Early in the game, it may be mitigated by an occasional casserole dish from a friendly neighbor. However, after time, most friends and neighbors begin to feel you have evidently found your way down the caloric path. That leaves you where? Gone are the days when your mate took charge of what appeared to be a mundane task of meal planning and preparation. If we only know what that implied, most of us would have been more empathetic. We would have passed up that bigger boat for our wife's desire for a remolded kitchen. Maybe that new stove was really needed! Or that supercharged refrigerator! We can't look back.

If you are a champ at grilling and carving (I was not proficient in either), you may have a head start on centering in on solving your daily gastronomic needs. I know some men who do all the cooking, but they are as rare as a cheap bottle of fine wine. If you fall into this category, fast-forward this chapter and move on to finances, laundry, maybe even sex for the single man!

If you are a pot and pans illiterate, then we need to put our heads together. If money is *not* a problem, the restaurant world is waiting with open checks. For money, you can enjoy anything from burgers to caviar, with lots of champagne to wash it down. If budget is a consideration, the answers are waiting to be discovered in that maze of pots and pans and mysterious appliances in your kitchen.

Before you analyze the situation, a word of caution: no matter where you dine—at home, at the IHOP, or the Ritz's Grillroom—you will initially be ALONE. Dining *without* a mate will be an adjustment for most men. There's no early and easy answer to ease this uncomfortable feeling. I've tried eating at home and watching the evening news at the same time. TV anchors can take up the silence but fall far short of being charming table companions. In a noisy and busy restaurant, I have often struggled to read a book. No matter what course I take, I'm still alone and feel the emptiness. In time, you will adjust and find your own pattern that fits your lifestyle. Eating alone may well be one of the most difficult adjustments you will be facing. One thought is to schedule the days you wish to have a reprieve from your kitchen duties by dining out with some friends. It really helps! A tip. You are a *single* man. Always make it clear you wish to cover *your* check so your friends will not feel obligated to pay for your dinner. An acceptable way to achieve this is to instruct the waiter when you order that you wish to have a separate check. You'll always be welcome that way.

> *I have enough money to live the rest of my life,*
> *if I don't buy anything.*
> —Jackie Mason

For most of us, eating out continuously is a drain on the budget. And a heavy dose of noisy dining spots has another adverse effect—being "overserved." It is far too tempting to sip *more* wine than needed or an extra cocktail or two while waiting for your order. Many sociologists point out that *excessive* drinking is a serious and detrimental side effect of widowerhood. It is so easy to fall into that liquid trap, and once in it, it's a high wall to climb over. Better that you try a combination of eating out and a do-it-yourself regimen at home with the heavy side slanted to "eating in." It is not as difficult as it sounds. But let's start with the simple stuff. No, not bacon and eggs (although they do have a proper place).

> *Part of the secret to success in life is to eat what you like and let the food fight it out inside.*
> —Mark Twain

For me, the first steps were a reconnoitering of my local supermarket. With our hurry-up world, with wives working full-time, a plethora of excellently prepared foods has come into being. Forget the old pork and beans of Granddad's days. Today, waiting for your shopping cart are exciting entrées ready for the microwave. You do have one I hope! There are roasts, meat loaf, fish, and even a selection of ready-to-go mashed potatoes with various additions like chives and even mashed sweet potatoes. Peek in the deli case for tempting shrimp, salads, etc.

> *Old people shouldn't eat healthy foods.*
> *They need all the preservatives they can get.*
> —Robert Orben

All rookies at shopping seem to make the same mistake—forgetting to make a marketing list *before* going to the market. In my first few excursions, I put two packages of frozen peas in my cart and discovered two more in my freezer when I got home. It will take me a month of Sundays to use them up. Remember how your mate always seemed to plan things just right, like the Japanese "just-in-time parts" manufacturing methods. Planning saves money and makes meal planning much more efficient. I try to plan for what I'll try to cook and prepare for the week. I'm becoming rather efficient on doing chicken thighs and legs. I have even had the courage to have several folks in for dinner with my "chicken Robert" as the entrée. The secret is to season the chicken before cooking, a heavy dousing of Lowry's salt and

McCormick's salt and spice adds zest. Under the oven in most stoves, you'll find a drawer with large boiling pans. Line the pans with aluminum foil. Folding up the corners to contain the cooking grease saves time on clean-up later. Broil the chicken for ten minutes on each side. If I'll be having one for tonight, I'll boil two more and freeze them for later. Saves on energy and my labor as another night's dinner is halfway prepared.

A revered source for quick meals is from the nimble mind and kitchen of Rachael Ray. My dear daughter by marriage, Gena, swears by Rachael's creations. Her books, like *Rachael Ray's 30 Minute Meals* (published by Lake Isle Press), are filled with mouth-watering entrées. Pick up a copy and away you go! Also, watching the Food Network's exciting performers will focus your mind into exploring the wondrous world of culinary exploits. I'm a real neophyte in the pots-and-pans venue, but I recently had the courage to entertain two couples with a four-course meal! Since they didn't suffer from food poisoning, I was invited back to their home for a delightful repast. Last night, I even produced acceptable eggs Benedict for an "amazed" lady friend. All of this is a part of my *work in progress.*

TO DATE OR NOT TO DATE?

It is strange that desire should so many ways outlive endurance.
—William Shakespeare

Let's start this often controversial topic with a few statistics. As we noted in the opening thoughts of this book, you, as a widower, are an *anomaly.* Here's the proof in hard cold statistics. The U.S. Census Bureau reports that almost 30 percent of women between sixty-five and seventy-four have lost a mate. This number climbs to over 50 percent of women between the ages of seventy-five and eighty-four. Over the age of eighty-five, more than three-quarters of women are left without a mate. And we have not even considered the millions of divorcées hunting for another acceptable mate. In a society where one out of every two marriages crashes, the number of what my parents used to call "grass widows" is enormous. Divorcées or widows, the numbers are on your side, so *where* do you start? And, more like it, *when?*

Sex Appeal . . . Give Generously.
—bumper sticker

We now live in a supposedly "relaxed and open" society, one that long ago relegated a "year of mourning" of our loved ones to the dustbin of history. You, older readers, may remember back when President Franklin Roosevelt wore a black armband for a year in memory of his mother's death. Much can be said about honoring the memory of our loved ones, especially our departed spouses. Grief is so individual that we will *not* go there in this book. These pages will be filled with thoughts to help you physically *survive* after your wife's death. If I'm any criterion, your heart will probably tell you when the right time is to venture into the mysterious dating milieu. Even thinking or saying the word "dating" will seem out of place at first, not to mention the act itself. My best advice is to frequently remind yourself that *you are alive*, living in the here and now.

> *A terrible thing happened last . . . NOTHING.*
> —Phyllis Diller

Depending on our circumstances, we all have an obligation to our children and close friends to pick up the pieces of our lives and move on. Remember how sad we felt as children when we learned from a delightful fairy tale that it was impossible to put Humpty Dumpty back together again? A friend of mine told me how her precious two-year-old niece picked up a handful of brightly colored fall leaves from the ground and asked her mommy "to put them back on the trees." Sadly, human time can't be rewound. Each day we have left is a *bonus*. Our lives as widowers are "live," and IT IS SHOW TIME! Whiners and those sitting on a pity perch will find the road they travel a bumpy ride, maybe ending up in a scrap heap with a broken Humpty Dumpty and a pile of leaves. We must all strive to come to grips with our heartbreaking losses and *move on*. I personally feel that breaking out of the "pity cocoon," and exploring a regenerated social life is the fuel that will jump-start our recovery from the greatest loss of our lives. And the fabric of a new social life will be woven with the smoothing comforts and warm friendships of attractive *females*.

> *There will be sex after death, only we won't feel it.*
> —Lily Tomlin

Yes, a *new* woman in your life, whether it now seems possible or not. As we are now rediscovering, the world around us is a *couple's* society. Two by two, during our marriages, we moved through years of high excitements and also years tattered with turmoil. But through it all, we always traveled through life with a soft, tender hand to hold and a support system that boarded on extraterrestrial! I'm referring to the incredible role our wives played as lovers, mothers, and best friends! Lest we forget, our wives were also the best guardians of our health, often the first to detect symptoms of health problems and then "nagging" to get us to see a doctor. Gail Sheely (more later) recently wrote the following in an article for *PARADE* magazine.

> A man who has a secure marriage and leads a sexually active life lives longer, succumbs to illness less often, and heals from wounds and surgery faster. Why? It all comes down to insulating a spouse from stress—regardless of whether the stress is physical illness or emotional stress, such as anger and anxiety.

The University of Chicago and Duke University also spotlighted the need for women in male lives. Their researchers reported that the *longer* a man spends as a widower, the higher his likelihood of developing heart disease or cancer. Add this to the mix. The same study reported that a widower has a greater risk of high blood pressure, diabetes, and stroke. That's enough to make any single man run to the first available matchmaker!

Perhaps by now the wonders of years past have started to become folded into a collection of treasured remembrances. Of course, the past cannot be simply erased from our current lifestyles, and there's no reason under the sun to try. Dating, dating, dating! Can it be?

Sex is good, but not as good as fresh sweet corn.
—Garrison Killer

I had been happily married for forty-one years. Exceedingly so! "Inseparable" hardly describes our life together. In my career as a filmmaker, we visited over fifty countries. Our busy social life was handled with trendsetting finesse. My wife's mothering skills were a marvel to observe. Yes, I admit Elizabeth was a saint in my mind and the minds of my children and friends. Replaceable? Of course not! Forget about *cloning* the women of our past. As you read this, let's take a long and healthy look at our lives right *now*, this *morning*, this *afternoon, tonight*!

A few paragraphs ago, we focused on the role our wives played in our physical health. That's only part of the story. How about our *mental* health and happiness? When my Elizabeth departed this earth, an enormous portion of the "best of my life" went with her—the dinners and parties, upkeep of a large home, and deep-seated relationships with our children only a mother can forge. I'm not mounting a "pity perch," just stating facts. You readers surely echo these thoughts. With Elizabeth's deadly cancer draining her physical being for many months, it was *a long goodbye.* One thought, one admonishment always shown through the sadness of departing. Since we knew *I* would be left behind, Elizabeth insisted I find a *new companion* within a reasonable length of time. I retorted it would be a miracle to find a companion with her qualities. Her reply was always "You can't live alone. You are too female dependent." That, my dear reader, applies to so many of us. Nothing to be ashamed about. In fact, I'm proud of the fact that I appreciate and will be dependent on the female of the species for a more complete remainder of my life. Ah, but locating and winning the object of this philosophy is another issue. And at my age, like the Bard said, "Time is of the essence."

In my heart of hearts, I sincerely feel that all wives who made this same *journey before* their husbands ended their earthly days wishing comforting championship for their left-behind mates, even those suddenly pulled from life without a long goodbye. After all, our wives loved us with their whole beings, and how could they not wish us happiness in the remaining years of our lives? Wouldn't we do the same?

Championship sounds so comforting when our pain of being alone seems to dominate every waking hour. But there's a flip side to companionship that must be put under a microscope. As an aside, Harry Truman once said, "If you want a *true* friend in Washington, get a dog!" That's not a bad idea, and many widowers have discovered the joys of canines. But we will assume we mean a charming, human, *female* companion. And now we are back to *dating*! Maybe we should use the term "market research." I am the first to admit that even holding a hand of another woman on my first forays in "market research" seemed a bit uncomfortable; it even felt like I was cheating on my wife. Physiologists tell us this feeling is a very natural reaction of a widower "coming out" into a marriage-driven society.

Take a look at our backgrounds. As husbands, we have deposited all our love and affection into a single source over the years of our marriages. That magical window is now closed! From this day forward, we are emotionally doing a *solo* fight. The controls will seem strange and the runway terribly long. Isn't there a good manual to help get off the ground? Some *CliffsNotes* to shortcut the course? *No*, we have to fly this sucker by the seat of our pants. Maybe we should think back for a moment to those mind-blowing apprehensions and overly protective concerns we had for our firstborn. How could we forget those nights when the baby would *naturally* cry and we both jumped out our beds thinking the end was near? And when the secondborn appeared, we handled parenting like a seasoned campaigner. Let the kid cry. Good exercise for his lungs! Well, try on the I-can-handle-it hat again and go forth!

UNDERSTANDING CONTEMPORARY WOMEN

Before you venture out, I recommend you read Gail Sheely's book *Sex and the Seasoned Women: Pursuing the Passionate Life* (published by Random House). It will give you a quick postgrad course in understanding today's "modern" women. Let's assume for a moment that you dated in college and maybe a few years beyond and you are now in your late sixties or early seventies—be prepared for a drastically revised, testosterone-driven society. For men of our generation (I'm seventy-eight as I write this), dating in today's world might be compared to Winston Churchill's comment about the old Soviet Union. As only Churchill could phrase it, "It is a riddle wrapped inside an enigma." And to many, so it is!

In the next few pages, we will try to untie the "gift wrappings" of what can become the most rewarding and exciting moments of your *work in progress*. Many widowers feel it is also the most effective method of healing the pain. However, before you read on, a *disclaimer* by this writer: I am *not* advocating "free love," promiscuity, or anything remotely resembling it. What you will read is my assessment emanating from interviews with ladies available for dating. You may take it for what it is worth. But keep in mind, the world is different today, and for many widowers, "dating" will be like venturing into uncharted waters.

Laugh and the world laughs with you,
snore and you sleep alone.
—Tony Burgess

First of all, most women you will find attractive have certainly enjoyed sex. After all, most of them have been married, often several times. I will put it this way. If *we* had enjoyable sex in our marriages, so did *they* in theirs. Hope that settles the morality issue. As we enter into the dating fray, we must erase from our minds the images of the Playtex girdle-protected girls we dated in our twenties supposedly fighting to retain their prized virginity for marriage. Even the movies of those times shouted out strict moral standards. If a film showed a *married* couple in a double bed, one of the occupants had to visually have *one* foot on the floor! Cleavage from heaving boobs was confined to those "dirty" magazines, hidden from mother and tucked away under our mattress. And, God forbid, condoms were requested (in a hushed voice) to a somewhat embarrassed local druggist. That was then, and this is now. Today's "seasoned women," to use Gail Sheely's appellation, are looking to enjoy life to the fullest. And that usually means an *active sex life*.

But wait a minute! What if you can't "perform" due to prostrate surgery or other medical deficiencies? Fear not, for many of the ladies you'll be attracted to have a penchant to "overcome." In case you've forgotten, there are exciting ways, other than penetration, to produce an organism. If this becomes "a riddle wrapped inside an enigma," time to visit you *local library*. It's a lot cheaper and perhaps more stimulating than an appointment with your urologist. I can't really visualize myself sitting before my learned urologist asking elementary questions about sex. After all, I'm a father of two and a grandfather of three! The puzzled doctor would probably recommend a visit to a specialist on dementia. Just kidding, Dr. Fernando Borges, (my urologist and a world authority on penile dysfunction and penile implants). We will explore this subject later.

> *I was married once, now I just lease.*
> —from the film *Buddy, Buddy*

Now, as we ponder our future path, we may have reached the proverbial fork in life's serpentine road. There's no global positioning system to electronically guide us to a worry-free Shangri-la. The decision we now face is to proceed with some sort of sex life during our "work in progress" or elect for celibacy. I'm not trying to be flip or cavalier about this choice. On the contrary, it is a serious condition that might well be colored by the vivid memories of the lost love of your life and the often conflicting attitudes of your children about "daddy dating" well-meaning advice from close friends and relatives, and your church. But it all boils down to *numero uno* time! Only you can call the play. It might well be "fourth and goal"! However, if we are ready to include *female* friends (perhaps lovers) in the remainder of our life, getting a handle on "what's happening" only makes good sense. At this time, I am assuming you *do* wish to join my troop and follow the trail that might reawaken our hormones. Believe me, you won't find hair growing on the palms of your hands!

> *Love is the only game that is not called on account of darkness.*
> —M. Hirschfield

For your first "trial heat" in contemporary sex education, I recommend your local library's vast storehouse of knowledge. Waiting for you in the library's stacks, under the Dewey Decimal system 305 code, are very helpful and descriptive books on this formally taboo subject. Remember when the Kinsey Reports were released? Demonstrators went wild demanding the book be burned! Heresy! "Back to storks and birds and the bees," was their misguided war cry. And the uproar over the "pill?" No matter what you feel religiously about sex education, it is available for all to read in the library's hundreds of titles.

Many will seem to require the reader to have a medical degree to understand all they import. Others have been written for guys like you and me. Just amateurs seeking to see what are the ground rules in today's sensual playbook. There are even *audio* books and Braille editions for the blind. Everybody has a right to know and enjoy this natural delight, right? Again, please remember my disclosure of not being an activist for free love or promiscuity.

> *Too much of a good thing is wonderful.*
> —Mae West

Look carefully left and right to be sure the coast is clear (you don't need to wear an 007 trench coat), stealthily proceed into the stacks and peruse the tempting titles. Then take out a few and settle in a quite corner for a fruitful read. Just to be safe, turn the books over so their covers aren't showing. You never know when a neighbor or a fellow church member might be nearby. As you turn the first pages you may have a flash back to your teen years. Remember when that brazen kid brought a cheap skin magazine to school? When you, as a man of the world, casually took a peek as the naughty pictures? The daring shots of glamorous looking girls posing in just their bra and panties! Wow! Today you can see the same thing and more on the tube hawking lingerie and sexual enhancements. Are we moving forward or not? I wonder.

As you begin to thumb through today's sex education publications, you begin to realize how "open" we have become. Today's generation didn't invent sex, but they apparently have a better understanding of the "birds and bees." Of course that's also very debatable, considering the astounding numbers of divorces and the escalating numbers of children born out of wedlock. The choice in the stacks runs the gamut of every aspect of sexuality. One title caught my attention, *The New Good Vibrations Guide to Sex*, written by two ladies, Cathy Winks and Anne Semans. These names must be noms de plumes! Give this effort a test drive. The author's mantra is easily understood: "Sex is good, clean fun, and the more we learn about it, the more pleasurable it becomes." Can't you hear the denials of the local bishop? Sex *without* marriage! It will never be right and proper! Come on guys, lets face it, the more we, as widowers, understand the sexuality of the new millennium, the more successful we will be inserting ourselves into the current climate of relationships between the sexes.

Back to *The New Good Vibrations Guide to Sex.* In these wide ranging pages you find everything you wanted to know and some topics that will make your ears tingle. Oral sex and masturbation are discussed in clinical detail. Cogent tips on initiating sex, and the beat goes on! Dr. Marc Nelson of Stanford writes in the foreword, "This book should be read by everyone—men and women, adolescents and elders, laypeople and professionals. It will significantly contribute to a person's heath and education." This book is only one of many I reviewed during my first trip to the 305 stacks. If you have a free afternoon, visit your local library. I'm certain you'll find some publications that will enhance your feelings on dating and sex!

Time to insert another disclaimer. If you are currently considering courting a lady in her *middle seventies*, her morality may be a throw back to her girdle restrained youth. In these cases just rewind time and march on! However, most widowers we interviewed stated they would prefer to enjoy the company of *younger* ladies and there's where some post grad courses are very needed.

> *Mahatma Gandhi was what all women*
> *wish in a man—thin, tan, and moral.*
> —writer unknown

It may come as a shock to you that many of today's professional, financially independent, well traveled, mature women will freely discuss sex early in dating encounters.

Remember, with AIDS and other deadly serious impediments, don't be surprised if the conversation subtly turns to exploring *your* sexual heath and past experiences. After all, widows and divorcées have often been married two or three times, and have certainly experienced the dalliances of the male species. In our interview with Cathy (not her real name), a very attractive, highly educated, salesperson, high school assistant principal, she bluntly stated that most women of her generation have a built-in fear of contracting a deadly disease during so called "safe sex." Cathy told me of her strong desire for sex, but added that her sensual drive is tempered by a need to know a serious partner's sexual history. How is this ascertained? Cathy just asks a potential sex mate about his past. Girlfriends, former wives etc. And from this she gathers the hints and salient facts she feels are essential before the gift wrapping comes off. No Lotharios need apply!

Another interviewee went even further. A very attractive retired executive flatly stated that many of her female friends (meeting a new man they had a sexual interest in) requested a current blood test as a safety valve for future relationships. All signs of our times!

This sensual inquisition can be a two-way street. You, in turn, should have a concern about the sexual health and past experiences of any ladies on your "might call list." Please don't let these information quests become too "Dragnetish." Remember Joe Friday's brittle voice uttering "just the facts please"? Joe (in less than thirty minutes of TV screen time) always got his pray to confess before the last commercial. But you are "live" in these situations. No commercials. No rush. In quizzing a lady fair, be a bit more subtle and charming. The real experts in this field admonish neophytes to keep in mind that divorced people are not exactly proud of the number of times they have been before a judge. So keep under the radar and under the speed limit. Rushing the sex speedometer in any relationship can get you pulled over fast. The great lovers of literature always kept their ladies a bit puzzled. If you cool your jets on the first few encounters, most ladies will begin to feel perhaps they must put a pedal to the metal.

> *The secret of staying young is to live honestly,*
> *eat slowly, and lie about your age.*
> —Lucille Ball

Seasoned ladies are not only sex wise, they can be aggressive. A cute, busty teller (in her early forties) at my bank sent me a valentine and always seems overly interested in my welfare. Maybe this is the bank's customer relation's policy, or am I becoming delusionary? That sets the focus on another aspect of widowerhood. Do we become *delusional* after the death of our wives? Let me explain what I mean. I have noticed that older women will often smile at me as I walk through a mall or shop in the local market. Two things might be a cause of this pleasant moment. Either I look like a *father* figure (I'm six feet tall with a shock of sliver hair) or I'm someone these ladies would like to meet. Egoism can easily blur your thinking as you grapple for an answer. In the effort to be unbiased, I checked with some wives of my male buddies. One of the wives I admire greatly told me, "There are lot of available women in today's world, and they are always unconsciously hunting for a relationship. You are passing by, and they may wish to make contact." Could it be? I haven't pressed the issue by verbally responding to unknown ladies during such moments. It would be embarrassingly catastrophic to misinterpret such a smile and be rewarded by a tap on the shoulder by a member of the store's security force. On the other hand, perhaps we are sending out a male pheromone trumpeting that we *are* available. This *illusory* topic will remain a mystery to me and, I'm sure, to many of my readers.

I recently have developed a very enjoyable relationship with a very attractive, well-groomed lady I originally noticed in a medical waiting room, perhaps the only pleasant thing that ever emerged from the countless *hours* I have spent contemplating my navel, waiting for a doctor to spend only *minutes* examining my condition. A few days later, I saw this same lady in my local supermarket and engaged her in a friendly conversation. She later told me she did notice me in the waiting room and might have even smiled my way. Does that count? The main thing is *she* called me a few weeks after the market encounter and asked me to join her for lunch. Calling a man for a date is not uncommon today.

> *If you wish a quite life, get a phoneless cord!*
> —unknown

A few thoughts on HMLs (high-maintenance ladies). If you encounter very well-dressed women wearing expensive jewelry, well spoken and well traveled, an HML may be in your sights. Don't panic. We, as venerable widowers, are easily attracted to these very desirable types. What's a good game plan? Best advice seems to keep a level head and think twice before you jump. Don't know if that helps, but it might make sense.

One day, long ago, I was at a dinner party at a very posh private club in Palm Beach. Seated next to me was an "overserved" elegant beauty (perhaps in her early forties) adorned with an incredible collection of emeralds—real, of course. The value of her necklace, rings, and earrings would probably rival the GNP of many small nations! As I admired her dazzling earrings, a thought flashed through my wine-soaked mind. If just one of the lady's emerald earrings fell into my wineglass, I could swallow it, smuggle it home, and live comfortably on the proceeds! Of course, nothing of the sort happened, and as the evening progressed and the Grand Cru wines flowed, this enchanting HML moved seductively close and whispered in my ear that she was on her *fourth* marriage. After more sips of wine, she informed me that her current husband (at the head of our table) would soon be battling with her attorneys for a very substantial settlement. With an unlined face (reflecting the skills of an expensive surgeon) and a captivating voice, she confided in me further. Pulling close to my face and looking right into my eyes she cooed, "My real concern about the forthcoming divorce is *not* money". This revelation piqued my interest. Then, looking carefully around to keep the atmosphere of secrecy she dropped the bombshell. Hubby number 4 is playing in the finals of the club's tennis championship, and her poor hubby has no idea a martial split is in his future. So flashing a 1,000-watt smile, the lady asked me, "Would a sudden and unexpected divorce summons upset my husband's tennis game?" That's real caring! I mumbled an answer that I didn't play tennis. With that she quickly assumed I didn't want to be in the finals for hubby *number 5* and turned to the man on her left for the rest of the evening. God love her . . . what a way to live a life, emeralds and all!

> *I am a marvelous housekeeper. Every time I leave a man,*
> *I keep his house.*
> —Zsa Zsa Gabor

If an HML is of interest to you, please pause and ponder if *she* can maintain the high maintenance on *her* funds, or will you be expected to be the main contributor? Women's high-fashion shoes alone could break the bank. A comic once said, "Any woman can get a good pair of shoes at a bowling alley for 85¢!" Try that number on Worth Avenue in Palm Beach. It won't even cover the parking meters. If your financial condition is flush, then there's no problem. If the contrary exists, then begin to make a subtle inquest into her finances. I don't mean a DNB, but there are ways to ascertain this information. Does she own her home? Check out the furnishings and the fancy car in the driveway. Chat about the stock market and where the trends seem to be going. Chances are that you will soon be well-informed and can elect to continue the relationship or bid the lady au revoir. Don't get me wrong. Many a delightful HML is also looking for companionship. And a new man in their lives doesn't need to be a close relative of a Rockefeller to qualify.

>   *Glory is fleeting, but obscurity is forever.*
>   —Napoleon Bonaparte

MEETING A NEW LADY

So if what we have covered to this point doesn't make you want to jump back in bed alone and pull the covers over you head, you're ready to hear the opening gun of the dating game. On your mark, get set. GO! Wait a minute! Where do the games begin? Where is the best arena to meet A-team women? The first playground you might think of is that cocktail joint your kids might have mentioned during their tussle with mate finding. Zero, nada, zip! These "meat factories" are for the lean and hungry thirty-to-forty set. These players know the rules and make the proper moves. In this rock-driven atmosphere, where deep cleavage is a part of the team uniform, you'd feel like an old coach who has been fired for losing too many games. I can recommend many other arenas where you will comfortably feel a part of the team.

A cruise ship, for instance, is a well-known catalyst for romance. But remember, you are a *single* person, and all fares are quoted "per person, *double* occupancy." If you wish to travel alone, cruise lines add a hefty surcharge for your cabin. The good news is that cruises, *without* single surcharges, are frequently available. Even the most upscale cruise lines are catering to this expanding singles market. Another thought. Try to avoid the "three-day drunkeries." Because of the cheap fares (often just a few hundred dollars), the passenger list is brimming over with "fast movers" out for a round-the-clock frenzied ride. If there are any widows on board, they may have poisoned their husbands for insurance money. Time for another Winston Churchill story. At a gala gathering, a pompous society lady said to Winston, "If I was *your* wife, I'll poison your tea." Winston replied, "If I was *your* husband, I'd drink it!"

> *It was a woman who drove me to drink,*
> *and I never had the courtesy to thank her for it.*
> —W. C. Fields

I would recommend that you "kick the tires" of a seven—to ten-day cruise. Many ply the Caribbean in the warm winter months. Also, these cruises are far less costly than the same-length itineraries offered in Europe and Asia. Again, check the Internet or call your local travel agency. These longer winter itineraries are very appealing to older (let's say "mature") ladies, often traveling in pairs. Question? How do you approach an appealing female in this setting? Please don't try "Have you been here before?" or, "What's your sign?" She might answer, "A *stop* sign," and walk away.

Meeting and mixing on a cruise ship seems to come naturally. Around the pool, in the many bars, just say hello and carry on from there. Keep in mind that the lady in your gunsight is also interested in meeting men and will often be very receptive to your conversational offerings. If you are really reluctant and might fumble the ball on the opening play, ask to see the cruise director. It is his or her job to "people mix." Every ship I've been on has extroverted cruise directors who host singles get-togethers. That's a tried and true gathering you may wish to attend. I know of many couples who met on cruises and lived happily ever after.

By the way, when reading the ship's newspaper of daily events, "Friends of Bill W" with a room and time will always be listed. That's a seagoing version of Alcoholics Anonymous. If you are afflicted, it's a great venue.

The best place to locate singles cruises is on the Internet using a search engine such as Google. Type in "cruises for singles." Up will pop dozens of interesting trips, many with little or no surcharge. If the cruise offered is part of a single's *group promotion,* try to check out the age profile of passengers. If the mean age is under forty and you are a budding seventy-year-old, *stay on the dock*! It's not to say that younger women on this type of cruise won't take a shot at you. Many thirty-year-olds, bored with their peers, might find a father figure very sexy and intellectually appealing. However, building a long-term relationship with this chronological spread is very risky. After the initial attraction wears thin, the older guy may be dumped for a young stud. Can we really blame the girl?

> *Go and never darken my towels again.*
> —Groucho Marx

So what's next? A church group? Yes, most major dominations have adult groups devoted to widows and widowers. It is true that many new couplings started among members. But it is not a dating service. We'll look at them later. Most groups of this type tend to focus on the *grief* of those left behind. If you are ready to "move on," you may not be receptive to reruns of your and the other's grief. I personally spent three months in a grief group, a part of the Hospice Bridge Program. Many of you may have experienced the incredible healing hand of the program during the final weeks of your wife's life. Their volunteers have made the difference in so many lives, allowing the ailing to die with loved ones in their homes. Unfortunately, my wife needed such high-tech medical care in her final weeks that it was impossible to move her out of the hospital to our home.

I would like to take a moment to reflect on the Hospice Bridge Program, designed to help the "left behinds" work through their grief and reenter the world. There are a number of programs, some for suicide grief, other for a loss of a mother, etc. I elected to join a group composed of seniors who lost a spouse. I was the only male thrown into a group of nine much-married and then much-widowed women. Some seemed to have more experience with funerals than many small-town undertakers. To my mind, too much time was spent on announcing to one another the fact that we are all in deep grief.

I suppose the reason behind this stems from the success of Alcoholics Anonymous, having new members *publicly* announce their affliction as a first step toward sobriety. I was looking for help to just physically survive and ways to pick up bits and pieces of my life. I remember one session when a heavyweight lady (a three-time widow) told us in a raspy voice about her main complaint. "I feel," she said, "that my married friends don't ask me to join them anymore because they're afraid I will steal their husbands!" To use my dear departed wife's Irish expression, "God love her!" Another lady spent most of a half hour giving us a detailed "organ recital" composed of a doctor-by-doctor, pill-by-pill rerun of how her husbands passed on, ending with a happy conclusion that her Tom died much better than her Bill. I sat there bewildered, wondering if a prize might be in the offing for the most beautiful death.

Please don't feel, however, that I'm downgrading the work of these groups. If you are a very recent widower, you may find welcoming solace in these venues. A hint might be to ask if the Hospice in your area has a group or knows of organizations composed mainly of widowers. This would have appealed to me in the early months of my mourning. I was seeking help on learning to handle household chores, advice on selling the family home, and when to start the possibility of a new social life. There well may be such groups in existence that covers these needs. I am aware of singles social clubs that are every gratifying for long-term singles. My thoughts are for the first months and first year.

HELP FROM COUNSELORS

Another invaluable avenue is to locate *personal* counselors. Hospice has some very good ones, highly trained to zero in on the sensitive needs of mourners. I was very fortunate to make the acquaintance of Ms. Karen Jones at the Hospice unit at the Palms of Pasadena Hospital in St. Petersburg, Florida. Karen took me under her caring wing even before my wife died. Being a widow herself, she provided comforting thoughts at a time when I most needed it. It was through Karen Jones that I became aware of the most frequent emotional booby trap of new widowers—a premature romance.

New and lonely widowers, she explained to me, are extremely vulnerable to unexpected and seemingly comforting emotional and sensual influences. She continued with the revelation that far too many recent "left behinds" become entangled in early romantic encounters only a few months after the death of a spouse. Often the object of the new affection could be a long time family friend. Perhaps a comforting member of the widower's church. Sometimes is might just be a chance meeting with someone that produced immediate shock and awe. But no matter what the source, far too often, these fresh-out-of-the box attachments have a very hurtful meltdown. If marriage occurred, the divorce rate is abnormally high. Karen stated that these unfortunate couplings are driven by the innate desire of a widower to quickly seek a *replacement* for his lost spouse, a natural desire to fill the huge void of an emotionally broken heart. "Wait for a *year* or *two* before making any serious moves," were the words that came from Karen's lips.

I listened but did *not* heed these sage words. I soon became enmeshed with an attractive out-of-state fifty-nine-year-old designer. After several candlelight dinners on romantic weekends, she confessed to have been married four times before the age of forty! Following this bombshell, I made the serious mistake of telling my children a bit of my new friend's life experiences, with the caveat that all seemed OK from my perspective. My family didn't see it that way and soon became very concerned that "Daddy was losing it to an unstable, fortune-hunting hussy." I'm still sure that this was not this lady's MOS. However, after a few months, the romance fizzled, and I became a dedicated adherent to Karen Jones's steadfast rule: "Wait a year before making any life-altering decisions." More very significant thoughts about informing your children about your romantic escapes later.

Also, I was surprised to discover that Medicare, in some cases, will cover the fees of a professional psychologist. My wife was in the final months of her life suffering from rectal cancer. During this stressful period, I was simultaneously diagnosed with colon cancer and required immediate surgery. A double whammy to say the least. My wife passed away in November, shortly after my colon surgery. I began a six-month chemo regimen and have recovered; my cancer is in remission. It was during my treatments that I was informed that my oncology group had a clinical psychologist on their staff, Dr. Patricia Burkett. Thus began a series of sessions (covered by Medicare) with the good doctor that has proven invaluable as I entered the enigma of dating again.

I recently had the opportunity to sit down with Dr. Burkett and explore some burning questions concerning relationships that will be faced by new widowers. In response to my question as to women's preference between a widower and divorcée, widowers came out on top. Why? Widowers are usually coming from a happy marriage that only ended with the passing of a spouse. Widowers also have a good track record of experience in the management of successful partnering. And most importantly, a widower usually has a better chance to smoothly integrate a new partner into his family circle. "A new lady that is kind and caring to Daddy" is normally very acceptable to his children.

A divorced male, on the other hand, usually brings a boatload of "baggage" with the strong possibility of an *ex*-wife often causing fault lines with the male's children and grandchildren. This is doubled in spades when the new *female* partner also has children by a previous marriage. Remember the old Hollywood gag, "*My* children and *your* children are fighting with *our* children!"

So it sounds like widowers are the winners by ten lengths? Not quite! What's the downside? Dr. Burkett warned of *"sainthood."* The overidealization of a departed spouse. This is a deleterious atmosphere that will hang like a wet drape over a new relationship, forcing the "new" lady to feel she is always trying to live up to a ghost. Keeping a healthy and honest memory of our departed will keep a new relationship moving forward on smooth waters.

Another concern of widowers is related to that timeless and ageless subject of, you guessed it, sex! As I mentioned in a previous chapter, we are entering a new cosmos as we launch the dating process. What will we encounter? Stand by for a major makeover. Dr. Burkett pointed out that the majority of *today's* attractive and successful women are coming from broken marriages and unsuccessful relationships. In today's parity-driven society, they establish their own personal *codes of moral ethics* to fit their current lifestyles. These codes vary greatly, and apparently there is not a set pattern of "right and wrong." In most cases, women in this age group are not bitter concerning men in general and are usually seeking a Mr. Right. In their search, **sex**—yes, good old-fashioned sex—is still on the front burner.

Dr. Burkett feels it is very important for any man to realize (in the beginning of any relationship) that most attractive and younger women will govern their lifestyles around their very personal codes of sexual behavior. If we, as widowers, wish to become "intimate" with a new lady, it is up to us to subtly scope out the guidelines of these codes. Much of any woman's sexual code hinges on such factors as previous experiences, self-esteem, physical health, compatibility, desire, frequency, style, and techniques. Dr. Burket's major admonishment is to steer clear of heavy drinkers, addicts of any kind, kinky sex demands, uncomfortable family circumstances, and serious financial problems. Any of these are tragedies in the making.

Underscoring all this, Dr. Burkett continued, are physical changes. Women after menopause undergo a major change in their vaginal region. Just as we men undergo changes in our "equipment," a thought to keep up front. Another major concern of today's attractive, socially active women is the "purity" of a male. With the HIV crisis, it is little wonder that *smart* women will often demand a blood test from any male they intend to be intimate with. Correct? Yes, and any of us might be faced with this as we venture forth. Don't be offended as you (after giving this some deep thought) may wish this matter to become vice versa!

I concluded my visit with Dr. Burkett by asking for her thoughts on missteps many new widowers incur. First and foremost in her mind were the dangers of *early romantic* entanglements. Most widowers, feeling so incomplete without a spouse, can easily take the bait of any attractive lady waiting in a "trial balloon." Remember my experience flying high for a few weeks? Fortunately, most of us learn from these sidebars and move on with our lives.

Always keep in mind that women of all ages have always searched for steady-minded and caring men. We, as widowers, have mostly come from successful and happy marriages. Only death ended our relationships. I feel, in time, each of us will find a new mate. Not a "clone" of the past, but an entirely new woman, with her own special characteristics. Hopefully, our lives will again be fulfilled, and the next stage or our being will have a wonderful story to relate.

CLONING!

Just a few words about the dangerous hallucination of *cloning!* All of us would give all we own to merely push a few buttons and out would pop a *perfect clone* of our dead wife. Remember the Frankenstein movies? Even Hollywood couldn't make a perfect clone with all the special effects in their cinematic bag of tricks! Remember the bolts in the monster's neck and his "loving" personality? Many years later, some movie types wrote a similar horror-filled script for *The Bride of Frankenstein*.

Frequent dreaming of cloning *and comparing* will only slow the healing of your grief and will certainly be detrimental to any relationship you might hope to develop with a female. Cloning is a "never-never" land bad dream. *Comparing* is even more dangerous because it is a bad habit we can *actually* practice in the here and now. Let's assume for a moment you meet and are attracted to lady A, the recent widow of Joe A. In a few social exchanges with lady A, you uncomfortably find yourself being compared to "dear *dead* Joe?" "Wonderful, talented Joe," his widow likes to remind any male, "could fix a complicated washing machine, even the air conditioner!" And you, my fellow widower, have trouble changing a light bulb! A little far-fetched, but you know what I'm getting at. No, you can never realistically recreate the past. You are (it's becoming a repetitious theme) a *work in progress* struggling to establish a reinvigorated life. If you wish any lady to comfortably share any part of your current lifestyle, please try to keep an open mind. It might hurt, but bite your tongue when you are tempted to compare lady A's burnt roast with your late wife's peerless cooking! I have strived to admire the unique personality traits and special talents of *new* ladies that have come into my life. In many instances, they have qualities my late wife *didn't* have and vice versa. But in all cases, I stay out of Frankenstein's laboratory!

ONLINE DATING

Another avenue to meet ladies is the Internet and its myriad of dating services. It is estimated that 62 million people are online every day. This proliferation of singles searching for their Mr. or Mrs. Good has resulted in a cottage industry of online sites. There's *Conservative.com* for those of the far right, *DemocraticMatch.com* for those of the left, even *Hannidate.com*, an online service promoted by talk show host Sean Hannity. *Match.com* boasts of a membership of over a hundred thousand. *ThirdAge.com* is another very popular service—upbeat, funny, and downright fascinating. Their mission is to bring men and women together in their "third age," whatever that is. There are also sites for Jewish and Christian singles. Also in cyberspace are many very questionable sites offering endless pictures and profiles of attractive foreign ladies waiting to be your next wife! As you well know on the Internet, as Cole Porter penned, *"Anything Goes"*! So handle your mouse with care! An astute writer described this online revolution as "transforming flirting into a 24/7 proposition." Click on Google and away you go!

For a modest fee, you become listed, and all you need to do is to stand by for the action. Online dating services can be very selective. State your age preferences and desirable proximity of possible dates. You will be asked to provide a "profile" of yourself. Education, income, physical factors, likes, and peeves—it all goes into a massive computer base somewhere and magically appears for the world to see. Like the old bromide says, "You may have to kiss a lot of frogs before you find your princess." A friend of mine said one of the online ladies he finally met in person was "a one-person slum." We'll try to spare you that fate.

I must admit, dear reader, that I tried two of these "services" to see where it would lead. In my forays, it was a dead end. After viewing the posted photos of the ladies and making several phone calls, I did arrange a tête-à-tête. A dinner with someone advertised as an attractive blond was a disappointment. Surely her Internet displayed photo was years old and her educational profile has been, shall we say, "altered" a bit. There was a total lack of chemistry to propel me to another meeting. One down and two to go. The second quest was to meet a British lady who explained her background as a well-traveled air hostess. On the phone, the accent and her knowledge of world destinations was intriguing. When we met, I looked at her face and body and came to the conclusion that her first flights might have been with the Wright brothers!

My third meeting was much more encouraging. The recipient of my phone calls and e-mails was a very attractive semiretired television network news writer and producer. Lunch was most interesting, as we had traveled many of the same paths over the globe. So one out of three is not too shabby. Sixty-two million people can't be wrong and many "onliners" have located and found happiness with a new Ms. Good. So fire up your old computer and sail forth into cyberspace and see what evolves.

Romance in cyberspace usually begins with a few e-mail conversations. You have the choice of hitting the delete button anytime the exchanges seem unappealing.

If all e-mails appear *de rigueur* on your monitor, you may next wish to exchange telephone numbers. You'll learn a great deal about a person through "live" phone conversations. A good opening question is to gently ask, "How recent is the photo you displayed on the Internet?" I felt that a few I met slipped in their high school graduation photo! That's stretching it a bit, but the fact remains that all of us look in the mirror and mentally erase our age "souvenirs." With a voice in your ear, you can quickly ascertain a lady's fluency, lifestyle, and perhaps key interests. If like to ride your Harley and she prefers sailing small boats, you may "Have a problem, Houston".

OK, let's assume you have located a lady you would like to get to know a bit better. If you have a fixed income, somehow allocate some funds for dating. Now is the time to bring to you, fellow widower, some "men's confidential." Approaches to this topic are pioneered by some very experienced gentlemen. And it all revolves around the costs of dating. I'm not making light of a serious situation. We'll start with taking a lady out to dinner. Face it, dinners are costly. A well-rated restaurant—with cocktails, wine, and the tip—is always in the range of $85 to $100. If you take her to the IHOP or McDonalds, the tab is less. But I am assuming that you are a better sport and wish to make a good first impression. The most reasonable, costwise, is meeting for a midmorning coffee at Starbucks. It sounds like a respectable place, and if you don't like the lady, you can always look at the books and magazines. If you're willing to wager a bit more, try lunches. The cost is half a dinner tab. And like the coffee idea, seeing a lady in bright daylight can be more revealing. And the same goes for you, my man! Candlelight is a wonderful wrinkle remover, but the out-of-pocket is much higher. Save that route for the ones who make the first cut. Most of the best restaurants in any area have luncheon specials that won't cost you an arm and a leg. Also, it is more "cool" to bypass expensive wines and cocktails at lunchtime (driving you know). Ice tea seems more natural and saves about half the cost of a "lushy lunch."

If you drink, don't drive, even putt!
—Dean Martin

Here's another thought: If you feel your digs are appropriate and you can operate the stove without burning down your abode, your next date might be to invite the lady to *your* home for dinner. If this "come see my pots and pans" seems a bit suggestive, invite another couple to ease the atmosphere. Cooking at home is a great budget saver, and the wines and cocktails costs a fraction of a bar tab. I feel it is socially acceptable to ask the lady to drive her own car to your house as you are busy in the kitchen preparing the feast. Easy-to-prepare meals have been outlined in the chapter on cooking. My best hint is to carefully set the table with your finest china and glassware. A dear friend of mine, Charlie Samson, always commented on our tables, which I always set. He said, "Put a few thousand of dollars of English china and Waterford on the table and a hot dog becomes a gourmet delight!" How true. And showing off your culinary skills is a real turn-on for most ladies. Light the candles, turn on the romantic music, and let the games begin!

BUT DADDY, WHAT WOULD MOTHER THINK?

This brings us to a very delicate and much-debated and often-misunderstood family concern. What will your children think about your dating? Questions range from, "Daddy, Mother's been dead only a few months!" "Shouldn't you wait a year?" "She is nice, but isn't she a bit young?" to "She's been married how many times?" "Did she or the husband cause the divorce?" "She has children!" And the inquisition goes merrily on.

My advice to counter this is *limiting* the amount of information you give your children about your dating. Spoon-feed them with little bits. Remember, they are grieving for their *mother*, and simultaneously, they have your best interests at heart. Of course, your estate is another factor. God forbid that a new woman will enter your life and strip you bare. Children may now feel they are the parents and you are the child. Children will also focus on *any* woman you date from "the baggage" viewpoint. How many kids does she have? Did she or her ex-husband cause the divorce? Will Daddy be able to handle a younger woman? All are very normal and valid concerns of a functional family. My grandfather married Ida, called "the battle axe" by Grandpa's children. And she did strip him bare financially before he died. I'm sure you may have similar horror stories that will quickly come to mind.

A good way to forestall "heartburn" from this topic (as mentioned earlier) is to spend a few dollars on a good lawyer to set up your finances in such a way as to *protect* your estate from all comers. Make your children or heirs aware of the protective barriers in your will. And make them realize you are *not dead* and a lively and healthy social life is your choice for the rest of your being. Emphasize that you *are* capable of handling yourself at this time and will use good sense in dating. After all, you can't get a women pregnant! And if all else fails, try this approach. Set them up with the fact that you have made contact with a lady *without* any baggage. The ideal mate. She will cook and clean and make no demands on your estate. However, she is only twenty years old and lives in Thailand! Try that for size!

THE *M* WORD

*If you want a place in the sun,
be prepared to put up with a few blisters.*
—Abigail Van Buren

Marriage—to be or not to be? Today's more elastic morals have made living together, cohabitation, a workable solution for many couples meeting later in life. The legal profession doesn't engender the concept, for little billable legal hours are needed for reworking trusts and wills. It is possible to "just move in and hang up your clothes." For this example, we'll assume the home is one that is owned solely by one or the other of the "partners" now living together in a state of marriage or electing just to cohabitate. The ownership and title of the home should *remain* in the estate of the owner-partner.

Now the couple has settled in. All is well for many compatible years. Fast-forward! Has the happy couple considered and prepared for events that will take place *after* one of the "partners" passes on? Let's face it, we are exploring marriage and cohabitation possibilities much later in life. If you elect to try either approach, please keep a few thoughts in mind. While sharing a house (either owned by you or your new partner), you may *jointly* purchase new assets such as furniture, additional dishes, even remodeling the structure itself. In these instances, an agreement *in writing* should spell out the disposition of these assets following the death of one of the partners—in most cases, a fifty-fifty split between the estates of the partners.

What happens if the surviving partner *remarries* and decides to *sell* the home? An agreement (executed prior to joining together will ensure that the proceeds from the sale of the house are added to the estate of the *original* partner-owner. Sounds too complicated? As stated earlier, it's best to consult a lawyer in the very beginning, avoiding lots of tussles in the end.

Here's a quick note about antiques and valuables acquired while married to your late wife. Include them item by item in any written agreement. Upon your death, you may will them *directly* to your children or specify that your surviving spouse (or partner) may use them until her death. Then they will pass directly to *your* children. In my case, my wife had a natural concern about a second wife outliving me and passing these valuables on to *her* children. A good lawyer can straighten all these out, saving a lot of stress in the end.

KEEPING THE OLD "BOD" TICKING

*The doctor can bury his mistakes,
but an architect can only advise his client to plant vines.*
—Frank Lloyd Wright

In the discourse on the *multiplicity* of roles our wives played in our lives, I touched on our health. Our devoted companions managed to squeeze into their busy lives the duty of being *health sentinels,* quietly monitoring our passage through this life filled with serious health complications. When suspicions arose, our wives usually were the driving force to get us into a doctor's waiting room. As we are now alone, this vital task is ours to take over, and we must not take it lightly! A splendid doctor (who has seen me through to remission of my colon cancer) is Dr. Andrew Peterson, oncologist on the staff of Palms of Pasadena Hospital, St. Petersburg, Florida. With an earnest tone in his voice during my recent office visit, Dr. Peterson expressed the most truthful assessment I have ever heard of mankind's endless struggle with disease. "If we live long enough, we get *everything,*" said the learned doctor. Wow! That's something to look forward to. So where do we line up to get "whips and chairs" to fight off the genes and germs ready to give us "everything"?

Please realize I'm not trying to assume the position of a health guru. Heavens no! Consider me as just another senior that has been exposed to serious maladies, dodging the "silver bullet" several times through the healing wonders of high-tech medicine. The surgery scars on my abdomen are my campaign stripes. In this nation with excellent health services, uncounted numbers of people are enjoying extra years owing their good fortune to great surgeons and dedicated general practitioners. And that brings us back to being our own sentinels.

Trusting that most all of you readers belong to the nation's most important social club (Medicare) and you younger widowers are covered with good medical insurance, we have many opportunities to gather an arsenal of "whips and chairs." Number 1 on the duty requirements of your *sentinel* role is *frequent checkups* of your dear old "bod." In my case, I have a history of heart disease, glaucoma, and cancer. How's that for a trifecta? To keep these "uglies" at bay demands frequent look-sees. For my heart, it's a twice a year checkup, starting with a comprehensive blood work, then measuring cholesterol level, checking liver, and other vital organs. From the miracle of laboratory analysis comes the news—"good or bad." If "bad" pops up in the lab findings, the pharmaceutical industry and your doctor are ready with some powerful answers that save lives!

For my cancer (colon and prostate), it is blood work, CAT scans, and now a colonoscopy once a year. I can't find the words powerful enough to urge *any* man over forty-five to have a colonoscopy every five years and, after seventy, every two years. A routine colonoscopy a year ago saved my life by detecting my colon cancer early. With incredible surgery by Dr. John Clark and a chemo program directed by Dr. Peterson, I now enjoy complete remission.

Our eyes may be the "windows of our soul," but ensuring their visual acuity requires maintenance beyond the ethereal. Like millions of other Americans, I suffer from glaucoma, a disease that, if left untreated, can result in loss of sight! However, glaucoma, thankfully, can be easily detected by frequent checkups with an optometrist or an ophthalmologist. In most cases, glaucoma can be kept under control with modern medications. In my case, I have been cared for by Dr. Kevin Greenidge, a board-certified ophthalmologist specializing in the treatment of glaucoma. Dr. Greenidge (on the staff of the

Eye Institute of West Central Florida) is adamant in urging seniors to have visual checkups. The good doctor said, "Over 50 percent of people suffering from glaucoma don't even realize they have the disease. Therefore, it is essential to have yearly checkups, not only for glaucoma (which is a silent destroyer of sight), but other serious deficiencies that can cause severe impairment to the eyes." To keep your "windows" clean and clear, be sure to add a yearly *visual* checkup to your list of heath care duties.

Again a disclaimer, I am not a specialist in *any* medical field. True, I have a creditable background of several *thousand hours* of sitting in drab clinic waiting rooms to my credit. Also, an advanced degree in "faithful patience" awarded to me for behaving properly while waiting to be recognized with that welcome greeting, "The doctor will see you now." Question? Why don't these well-paid folks keep a more up-to-date collection of reading materials in their establishments? Haven't you suddenly felt "clairvoyant" when reading *Time?* Then after checking the cover, you realize it is *several months* old! Same for *People* magazine reporting the antics of Hollywood's cooing love birds when you *secretly* knew their lawyers are now battling it out? And how about these blaring TV sets offering endless commercials for new drugs and treatments? Thankfully, all is forgiven when we finally meet the doctor (often pressed to the wall for time) and receive expert medical help.

With the above disclaimer in force, here are a few thoughts about sexual desire. Experts tell us that all males occasionally experience the loss of desire for sex. The medical term is inhibited sexual desire or ISD. With the traumatizing loss of a mate and all of its associated physical and psychological factors, many new widowers may experience ISD. Answers lie in consulting a urologist, sex therapist, or other appropriate specialists. With today's advances, there is no reason to suffer from the pangs of ISD.

Another hush-hush acronym is ED, shorthand for erectile dysfunction, or simply impotence. Again, referring to experts, occasional ED is commonplace among men of most ages. However, as widowers, we have suffered through severe emotional stress, and this will impact performance. Increased drug and alcohol usage is also a deterring factor. Medical authorities state that approximately one-third of ED cases are psychological; one-third, physical; and the remaining third, a mix of both cases. Your urologist has the answers in all cases. If you wish, use Google to locate the Web site of Dr. Fernando Borges, a world authority on ED and an innovator of penile erectile systems.

Most medical plans initially direct you to a primary doctor who in turn will refer you to specialists if needed. On any route you wish to take, it is vital that *you* become the sentinel of your own health. It seemed so simple when our wives were on guard duty. Those days are past, and we must man the ramparts! Just keep in mind Dr. Peterson's prophetic utterance: "If we live long enough, we get everything." Let's all raise our hands and swear to be vigilant and proactive to keep all our parts humming along. Our children, grandbabies, maybe even *great*-grandbabies are counting on us!

DOLLARS AND SENSE

When you don't have any money, the problem is food.
When you have money, the problem is sex.
When you have both, the problem is health.
—author unknown

Believe me when I tell you that I am not a financial expert, far from it. But with the performance of the stock market and the up-and-down quirks of the economy, who is? Brokers and stock peddlers certainly like to assume the pose of having *intuitive* powers, but aren't they looking into the same crystal ball as we do? However, most of us with a few bucks left after educating kids and paying off house mortgages turn to them to help guide us. Bless them all, and here's a toast to their intuition! May a few bucks drop into my cup!

Our individual financial situations are as different as our DNAs. I wish only to skim the surface with a more pragmatic viewpoint of our fiscal housekeeping. If you (as a couple) received social security (a blessing that flows from the Fed *for the moment*), you have already faced the disturbing fact that your income *dropped* by a significant percentage when your wife died. Your love's SS check (assuming she had one) is now absent from the mails and, sadly, your bank statement.

So in view of your altered circumstances, what should you do with your financial holdings? Experienced financial planners I talked to about this all seemed to agree on one path—DO NOTHING FOR A YEAR! Just sit tight for the first twelve months and see how your new pattern of life takes form. One myth always seems to surface. Due to the absence of your wife's *personal* expenses (hair styling, nails, clothing, etc.), there will be significant cost reductions in your monthly budget. Nada! Most folks tracking their expenses discovered the supposed cost reductions were offset by the widower's *increased* personal expenses—cost of cleaning the house, increased laundry bills, meals out of the home, dating, etc.

My advice is to track one monthly expense down to the penny. If you have a credit card, *charge* everything to it for a month. Groceries, gas, movies, cleaning—the works. At the end of thirty days, you'll have a better financial focus on where you stand. I did it, and it was most revealing. Beyond my *fixed* living expenses, I was spending *more* on the *nonfixed* expenses than we did when my wife was well and handling the costs of running the house.

Another thing, all the financial wizards mentioned a need to have an attorney *read* your *present* will. In most cases, our entire earthly wherewithal was in "joint tenancy" and passed (without probate) to us as the surviving spouse. Now, with you as the sole owner, it is time to make sure (in the event of your death) that your estate ends up *where* you want it. If you neglect to set up a will naming your heirs, the officials of the state you live in will make that determination. You have read of cases where beneficiaries (and *hopeful* beneficiaries) fought costly court battles to get their hands on the spoils. Many a famous and wealthy man has passed on *without* a proper will. It is so easy to forget this detail as we grieve. However, with the death of our wives, we do realize that death *can* come at the most unexpected times. Be ready for any eventuality. In my case, my will has been structured to pass my estate *directly* to my grandchildren, earmarked to help finance their education, a gift that keeps on giving. If I remarry, this will and its provisions remain in place, and the monies left in the estate move in the direction I wished in life. I'm not promoting business for an attorney, but this is a must!

When you are ready to revisit your financial picture, expert money people are there to advise you with many solid approaches. Annuities, life insurance, mutual funds—I'm sure you know the list.

However, I would like to repeat what all these financial gurus told me, don't do anything for a year.

SELL OR STAY

A huge concern for me after the death of my Elizabeth was, should I *sell* our home and move on? Here in Florida, the housing market was going through the roof. I'd make a sizable profit if I sold it. But wait a minute? First thought is, *where* would I go? Closer to my kids? A smaller place? Both seemed reasonable until I sat down and began to consider all the issues related to this major change in my life.

I'm sure that many of your readers have lived in the same house for many years. The physical effort and mental strain of a move shortly after your wife's death is something every counselor says we must avoid. "Wait a year, maybe two," they all pleaded. And for good reasons. Let's start with the *where* issue. Realtors tell me that many a sale is made to a widower (moving shortly after their wife's death) to be *closer* to their children. A very understandable reason. However, if you are considering this, also stop to analyze another human factor. When you move into a *new* town, all of your dearest and most helpful friends will be left behind. In most instances, these friends have been our main moral support as we struggled through the early days and months of our pain emanating from the death of our spouse.

Also, give this some serious thought. Our children (although they love us dearly) have their own lives to lead. When we move into their surroundings, we might be "a fish out of water." In a new town, it will take time making new friends of our age and rebuild our personal infrastructure, clubs, churches, medical doctors, etc. That's a lot to bite off in our later years. Yes, our children will try their very best to accommodate our needs for companionship. However, viewing it from their perspective, we might be asking too much. Give these some deep thinking and see where you end up.

In the first few months after Elizabeth's death, I spent every weekend with my children. Now, (almost two years) after her passing, I try to give them a break, cutting my visits to a few weekends a month. Maybe just a Sunday afternoon for a home-cooked meal and a tussle with the grandbabies. Although we raised our children to adulthood, they are really the products of another generation. That also goes for their close friends. If you don't think so, listen to *their* music! Remember when we loved boogie-woogie and Frank Sinatra while our folks listened to that "awful" Wayne King or Guy Lombardo on the *only* radio in the entire house! Ugh! It will take a serious bit of diplomacy to harmoniously blend our generation's desires and habits with theirs. Are you ready for that 24/7? On the flip side, many a widower has found happiness this way. But others discover that where they "were" best fits their needs and move back.

A SEA OF BOXES

Every one of us has "moved," perhaps more than we wish to remember. Besides the sea of boxes, this undertaking is costly, very costly. Check out some prices with local movers in your area. Spending $1,000 for a *local* move seems to be just the opening bid. An o*ut-of-town* move is in another league. To move from Milwaukee to Clearwater, Florida, in 1977 cost us almost $10,000! And we found that the moving costs where just the beginning!

As you look around your domicile now, the number of unused rooms seems to scream, "Downsize!" I had the same thoughts after realizing I'm only using the den for TV watching, the kitchen for meals, and the bedroom for sleeping. Why pay for the upkeep of a large living room, dining area, and guest bedroom? Yes, it *is* time to *downsize*! Tilt! Rewind! Rethink! *Downsizing sounds* great on the surface. But from a practical viewpoint, there's much to consider. First of all, let's consider our furniture. If you are now living in a rather spacious home, your furnishings reflect the roominess—large comfy couches and wonderful easy chairs, big dining room tables and chairs, bedroom sets with spacious dressers and end tables. But in a smaller setting, most of these beautiful furnishings will seem out of place, just too gargantuan for a downsized setting. Answer? Sell or give away most of the old and purchase new. A major hit on the budget!

Used furniture is a drug on the market. Take a few minutes to visit a good *used* furniture store. Checking the prices, the dollars you laid out for all your lovely pieces will seem like a bad dream. Then make the same fact finding to a *new* furniture store filled with pieces that will fit perfectly in a smaller setting! Ouch, the costs! Score another point for the folks who say, "Stay where you are for a year or two." Good advice, for we never know what tomorrow holds. For many, an ideal female companion might just walk into their lives.

Back to the more mundane issues of moving. If you have lived in a semitropical climate and you are contemplating moving north to cooler climes, be prepared to invest in some warmer duds! I well remember when we moved from Milwaukee to Florida. Anyone interested in a good deal on a used mink coat? The day I sold my snowblower before we moved was the most rewarding day of my life. I don't even like snow on a Christmas card! So after all my rambling, we come back to the basic question. Move or not to move? One alternative is buying four airline tickets a year and see the kids in that sequence. Like Fox News, "I report, you decide!"

KEEPING HOUSE AND HEARTH TOGETHER

When John Deere markets a riding vacuum cleaner,
then I'll clean the house.
—author unknown

Have you had the courage to peek into the closet where all the cleaning supplies, mops, and broom are stored? That's the *low* technology that your wife dutifully applied to keep your place livable. To clean or not to clean, is that *even* a question? While we ponder this dilemma, the makers of cobwebs and an army of dust mites are having *the best of the best* in the corners, slipping happily under the beds, even daring to reach under the frig! Isn't it a wonder how quietly and effectively your wife battled these creatures and won! Now, *we* are the generals in this *never*-ending war!

Maybe you have always had a cleaning lady or commercial service. Keep them on! Dependable, loyal cleaning ladies are as rare as a complimentary fifty-yard line ticket for a Super Bowl. Realizing that there was now little "traffic" in my house, I adjusted the times of my cleaning doyen from weekly visits to two a month. Works very well and saves on my budget. She had been with us for fifteen years, always on time and so trustworthy. Don't know how I'd handle the house without her loving care. A thought: please make sure your lady *knows* she's appreciated. Holiday gifts and *sincere thanks* each time they come to clean fuels their hearts and loyalty.

Let's assume your wife did all the cleaning in your abode—*solo*. And you have a "thing" about taking over the job. Time to investigate reinforcements. One approach is asking the wives of your good friends if they have a *private* cleaning person you might be able to hire. "Private" ladies are often less costly than well-advertised cleaning services. However, if a *bonded* service is of interest, check out "cleaning services" in the yellow pages. They have clever names: Royal Maid Service, Merry Maids, European Maids, Adam's Maids, Clean Sweep; behind the snappy name is usually a licensed and bonded service with literally an army of smartly uniformed personnel. All this "front" is, of course, hidden in the charges of their services. Best advice is to call several services and get a *free* estimate to keep your digs tidy. Also, be very specific about your particular needs when dealing with these folks. Do they reach up to high places like the tops of cabinets? Some will not allow their people to work over three feet above the floor citing insurance restraints. Is cleaning the *inside* of a refrigerator out of bounds? It is too easy to forget, dear fellow widower, that appliances need TLC, including cleaning *under* the refrigerator. That's why they come factory-equipped with rollers. Speaking of these miracles of cold storage, keep a sharp eye on *leftovers* stored in them such as that tasty casserole your kind neighbor brought in a few days ago. Or that gummy dessert that looked like it was made with chocolate steroids. Sure, we all have good intentions to use these goodies for lunch or dinner "tomorrow." For me, too often, that "tomorrow" just seemed to slip away. I have learned the hard way that leftovers morph into aggressive, pungent *green walkarounds* when ignored for long periods.

Of course, you can save some real bucks by tackling this cleaning "opportunity" all by yourself. You men who have helped your lady with these chores will already know most of the ropes. For beginners, you might ask your daughter or the wife of a good friend to give you *hands-on training* to operate a boom and mop and the other *low-tech* tools of the trade. Don't laugh! My daughter showed me how to run our washing machine and dryer just *yesterday,* nine months after my wife's death! My cleaning lady comes twice a month, and the laundry was piling up. So I now have a new MOS—an experienced washer and dryer operator! Maybe there's an income stream there!

A CLOSET OF MEMORIES

I'm rather certain all widowers will zero in on what this section connotes. Without looking, I'll wager that in every widower's home, large and small, is a closet filled with the memories of a beloved wife. In my case, in the first months after her death, it took on a feeling of a euphoric *shrine*. Each piece had a vivid remembrance tied to the happy times she wore it. Standing inside the closet was the start of a sentimental journey in my mind, recalling the fun times we shopped together to find just the right dress. On this hanger is the ideal suit for the "mother of the bride," a highlight of our daughter's wedding. Over here is a rack of spectacular evening gowns for the formal nights on our cruises. I can still hear the dance music and champagne corks popping. Can't help smiling at Elizabeth's collection of funky hats and the horde of shoes she adored. Wherever I looked, every item seemed to take on a life of its own, recollections that often brought tears to my eyes. Isn't there a similar closet in your home too? A question for all of us: when is the proper time to *close* the shrine and move on? Again, this is a very sensitive and highly personal decision. I'll try to focus on what worked for me and, again like Fox News says, "you decide."

If I may digress for a moment, the *when* in my case is linked to a devoted man of the cloth and a special friend, Father Gerard MacAulay. During the long and lonely heart-wrenching hours in a bleak hospital waiting area, Father MacAulay was always there helping us through the vigil. When death came, he was a rock to turn to. So it was only natural for me to ask this kind priest about the proper time to close Elizabeth's "shrine" and move on, especially *who* should help me? Father MacAulay suggested asking my daughter Bridget come to the house when I'm *not* there and start the procedures. The *when* for me turned out to be seven months after her death.

Bridget and her mother-in-law arrived one Saturday afternoon and gathered the clothing into bags. A few days later, I dropped off a full load of bags at the nondenominational religious organization operating a fine thrift shop. Now, the shrine is closed, and some happy souls are enjoying the excellent taste of my beloved Elizabeth. Having my daughter touch the clothing and bag them was a right choice for me. It is best that you ponder the issue in your mind. The bottom line is it must be *done* for you to move on.

BILLS, BILLS!

A carefree couple, living well beyond their means, regularly received many dunning letters from creditors outlining their stringent credit policy and requesting immediate payment. In time, the couple worked up a letter of reply, carefully explaining *their* family credit rules. The letter read, "Once a month we put all our bills in a wash tub. Then we have a big party and dance around the tub, pulling out just *two* bills for payment. If you don't stop sending your insulting and demanding letters, we will cease putting *your* bill in the tub!

My loving wife was a whiz at writing checks (on time) to cover our monthly bills—condo fees, utilities, insurance premiums, church pledges, just to name a few. For the first few months after her death, I either "lost" or unconsciously ignored these requests for payments. Creditors are not sympathetic to our personal loss, and late payments or no payments at all will put a serious hole in credit ratings. Perhaps you have the "I can't forget to pay the bills" syndrome plaguing you. My solution came to me when a person at my local bank mentioned *automatic* bill payments, sent out exactly on time directly from my account. Presto! The problem was solved. No late payments or late fees. Credit rating was protected. To enjoy this relief reducer, just ask a friendly face at your bank or most any financial institutions.

While on the subject of money and credit, here is another serious consideration: as widowers (in the grief and healing stage), we are the ideal target for slick hustlers and fraud experts. My dear wife, in her final days at home, received a call from a smooth male voice notifying us of his "organization's" investigation into the possibility of fraud in our checking account. For helping this organization (the National Fraud Investigation Bureau) to detect fraud in banking, we would receive a prize worth $500! It all sounded very official. Weakened by the influence of heavy medications, my wife complied and gave the "sincere gentleman" the numbers of our account. Within twenty minutes, using an ingenious wire transfer technique, hundreds of dollars were stripped out of our account. So please be wary of *anyone* requesting information and promising a "prize."

They are the most miserable of thieves, cleverly stealing millions from unsuspecting, vulnerable widows and widowers during their time of grief.

The number of Americans experiencing the horrors of *identity theft* has surpassed 27 million with the incidence rate increasing every year. The Fair and Accurate Credit Transactions Act (FACT Act) helps reduce identify theft. One provision requires the three major credit reporting service to provide consumers with a *free copy* of his or her personal credit report. You can obtain yours by contacting *www.annualcrediterport.com* or calling 877-322-8228. In this way, you can trace your credit activity and quickly note any fraud. If detected, you can place an *alert* on your credit files, notifying potential creditors to proceed with caution when granting credit.

Experts have developed excellent rules to help stop this crime:

1. Do not give out financial information such as checking and credit card numbers or your social security number, unless you know the person's organization.
2. Report lost or stolen checks immediately. Your bank will stop payment on them.
3. Notify your bank of any phone messages or mailed promotions (under the guise of investigating possible fraud) requesting your checking and saving account numbers; offering a valuable prize for your help.

4. Closely guard you ATM personal ID number and ASTM receipts.
5. Shred all financial solicitations and bank statements before disposing of them.
6. If regular bills fail to reach you, call the company to find out why.

FINAL TRIBUTE?

In the first year of my love's passing, I also faced the hefty costs of a dignified *final tribute*. I requested cremation for my love (her wishes) and a niche for her *ashes* in a local Catholic cemetery. My niche for my future ashes is there beside hers, prepaid! I won't delve into the details of the funeral. Psychologists always seem to maintain that funerals offer "closure." Perhaps this is true for personal friends and immediate family. My feelings run counter. Can *one* day, *one* event offer "closure" on a most wonderful life?

If I may digress for a moment, I would like to mull over another perspective on funerals. It might be way "out of the box" to link your wife's funeral with your *marriage*. However, there are parallels. I'll start at the beginning. My marriage (circa 1964) took place in Hollywood, California. Standing at the back of a small Episcopal church (and holding me up) was my good friend, Harvey Korman (remember him from *The Carol Burnett Show*?). As I was staring ahead in a sort of trance, Harvey said, "It's showtime, friend, and *you're* on." Propelled by his gentle shove, I marched forth and finally married the love of my life. I might add our "courtship" ran for over four years, back and back over the Atlantic Ocean, from Milwaukee to her native home in Ireland, even to Russia, Egypt, and, finally, to this little church in California. The clincher for this reluctant bachelor came several months before when my wife-to-be told me, "If you don't marry me, you will be making the biggest mistake of your life!" Wow, that was a "closure."

Perhaps you will agree with my belief that there is a cognitive *link* connecting the *ritual* of the *beginning* (the marriage) and the *ritual* of the end (the funeral). Recall your wedding for a moment. Did you, as the groom, before the ceremony, feel a bit spacey? Your body seemed present and ready, but your mind seemed to be out in space? Your wedding was indeed a special moment, a major *ritual*, your *first* step into a *new* life. A "closure" for your single days. Keep that thought for a moment.

Our lives are filled with the excitement and recollections of *rituals*; in college, it was joining a fraternity and, hopefully, graduation. If you served in the military, the rituals are for awarding medals, promotions, and recognitions. Then *within* our marriages, the *ritual* of baptisms, graduation ceremonies, and our children's' marriages. All are *rituals* that became part of the fabric of our lives.

Now, close your minds of today's surroundings and think for a moment about the *ritual* of a funeral, your wife's funeral. At this *ritual*, did you have a separation of body and mind, a momentary loss of reality? I know I did. I sincerely feel there is a link, a tie to our marriage ritual and the funeral ritual of our beloved spouse. Macabre? Maybe. For me, it was a beginning and an end, and that helped me to better cope with this life-altering transition, the alpha and the zeta of a wonderful coupling.

But I'm also the first to realize that a true "closure" after death is a "sometimes" thing. One day it can be *very* vivid, and on others, *very* ethereal. So far away! No manual, no timetable, no dependable answers. Writing this book has become a catharsis for me. More *work in progress*. But then, this is such a personal mater that you may want to put this book down and reflect on the above. When you're done, read on, dear reader. There's *much* more to come!

> *Middle age is when you have met so many people that every new person you meet reminds you of someone else.*
> —Ogden Nash

Let's go back to some of the thoughts we covered in the section, "Dollars and Sense." With the costs of a funeral and the loss of your wife's Social Security check, the first year of our widowerhood has a financial downstroke. If you have a comfortable retirement plan in place, great, my man, and cruise on! However, many readers will not be so fortunate, and a caution flag may be waving. Boston College researchers have devised a "national retirement risk index." The scary bottom line is that people retire today with an average of $60,000 in their 401Ks! Note that $60,000 has only *four* zeros. I repeat, *four*! Widowers in that category will soon be faced with a dilemma of trying to make both ends meet with perhaps only a Social Security check to hold them up. Why do I include this gloom and doom in this survival guide? Just a word of warning. As you are consciously (or unconsciously) looking for a new mate, be sure you understand *their* financial status. If the lady intended is attractive and comfortably well-off and you have a fine nest egg, then, wow! Much like two profitable companies *merging* to make a better whole.

> *Never invest in anything that eats or needs repairing.*
> —Billy Rose

"Merging" has some very positive features. Splitting the costs of living and leisure activities is not to be taken lightly. But unlike the spontaneity of sexy kisses in moonlight, "liftoff" will be a matter of delicate and careful planning. Many couples electing to "cohabit" will keep their existing estates *totally* separate, sharing only day-to-day living expenses and the cost of holidays. The legal term is no "comingling" of assets that exist at the time of this union. Any asset you acquired *prior* to a new marriage or cohabitation (*not* comingled during the new relationship) will be exempt from any legal claim by our new partner in the event of a breakup. In many states, comingled assets will be divided fifty-fifty. If you decide to move into the other's existing residences, then the deal will seem less complicated. However, if you decide to start "fresh" and *purchase* a property together, call a lawyer pronto. More about that later.

> *Believe it or not, all lawyers were children once.*
> —unknown

If you feel the need to have a *legal* joining (thankfully, still called *marriage* in the minds of most of us), then a lawyer will be absolutely necessary to help you join hands. Don't forget a priest or minister! A pre-nup (sounds like a colorful Caribbean cocktail with a little umbrella) is a sensible and safe way to ensure that what monies you both have will (in the event of the death of either of you) flow in the right directions. Most attorneys will advise you that this is also a proper time for both of you to completely reveal your financial situations. Disclosure of all assets available as a couple, determining prior assets to be set *outside* the new union, content and direction of current wills, and monies you wish to comingle for daily living expenses. And God forbid, in the event of a "meltdown," all your major assets will be properly and safely allocated. Sadly, a high percentage of second marriages and cohabitations do not survive. So it is a wise man that uses good legal help to keep mind and body together.

With the lawyer at the helm, it's also time to settle (before either of you leave this earth) the final disposition of your and your new love's assets—*other than money*. Antiques, special pieces of furniture, paintings, sliver, dishes, etc. Keeping it all "out in the open" will be a pacifier to those left behind. Bear in mind that few second wives enjoy the love and confidence that your first wife had with your children and their husbands and wives. It's just the nature of the beast and no reflection on your choice for a new mate. If you both come to grips with this fact early in the mating game, a lot of heartburn can be eliminated.

As I stated, I'm *not* a financial advisor. What I have mentioned are just some pragmatic thoughts of an observer of life. We, as widowers, are very vulnerable to the opposite sex at this stage in our grief. Falling in love can impair our vision. Remember the Bard who said, "Falling in love *blinds* us, marriage *opens* our eyes!"

BEING A *SINGLE* GRANDPARENT

Old age is when your liver spots show through your gloves.
—Phyllis Diller

Ready to make ready for another readjustment being *solo* as a grandparent? My three grandchildren (six-year-old Aidan and three-year-old twins, Liam and Maura) call me Papa. I'm sure your grandkids also have a pet moniker for you. Maybe it also is Papa, evidently running a close first as the most popular. For "Papa *widowers*" like us, the blessings emanating from grandbabies are far beyond my meager ability to put it into words. I'm sure you all agree that just holding and cuddling our little ones can momentarily ease the fervent pain of losing our loving spouses. These little God-given wonders will look at you with incredible innocence. Their uncluttered minds, pouring out astounding words and expressions, seem capable of competing with the fastest commuters. If you have the privilege of little ones in your life, take very opportunity to tap into their beings. Hold them and love them! Healing medicines haven't been created that even come close to a grandchild's unlimited love and compassion.

Wait a minute! I should also include *great*-grandchildren. Many of you readers are maybe into another generation of greatness. If so, everything that follows also applies to you.

WHERE'S GRANDMA?

As a *widower* grandparent, our new relationships with our children and their children may need some fine-tuning. Long before your beloved wife passed away, I'm sure you both began to enjoy the dividends of your many years of dedicated financial and moral contributions made to ease your children's entry into the adult world. Remember all those challenging years of praying that our children would grow up and prosper, creating a happy and functional family of their own? Now my children (and sincerely hope also yours) are totally independent and thankfully prospering. In my case, a boy (Kevin) and a girl (Bridget) were thankfully transformed by time and education into bright, productive young citizens. I'm so proud (and I'm sure you are too), I'm busting my buttons. Of course, a few pounds around my midsection have added to the image of "busting." But through it all, the results have been A plus. In Kevin's home, three more beautiful little ones carry on the Swanson name. As of this writing, our daughter Bridget (happily married) is "mothering" an expensive horse.

So how is it different being a *widower* grandparent? Maybe a *great*-grandparent? What first comes to my mind is "a feeling" that will become apparent at family gatherings you attend shortly after your wife's death. I realize that "a feeling" is rather ambiguous—nothing negative, but it *is* different. The love of "Papa" is always there as before, but *you* may initially feel emotionally *empty* arriving without your spouse. After all, grandparent outings were a *two-person* act. The memories of these precious events will take a long time to fade for all concerned. Perhaps the most vivid memory for the entire family will be "Mema's arrivals" (*Mema* being another pet moniker), always an exciting moment frequently centered on a basket filled with mouthwatering contributions for a delicious feast. The goodies were so appreciated by Gena (my beloved daughter-in-law), continuously struggling with the never-ceasing demands and needs of three little Swansons.

I must take a moment to voice my strong aversion to the term "daughter-in-law." Was Kevin's lovely wife, Gena, incubated during an irrevocable judicial pronouncement of a dispassionate, stoned-faced judge? Of course not! How about "daughter *through happy* marriage"? Sounds rather warm and fuzzy. Works for me! Contact your Congressional Representative!!! This issue supercedes some of the nutty issues they spend our tax dollars pondering on!

Back to the kitchen action. With the much-anticipated arrival of "Mema's" magic food basket, there developed an inseparable bond with Gena and the brood under her supervision. My responsibility was providing a bottle or two of companion wines and a good time was had by all! Naturally, with Elizabeth's passing, some of this exuberance faded. "Papa" was now on his own. I always thank the Lord that my family was there and willing to hold me up through many early weekends I was alone. I was blessed with the fact that the entire Swanson tribe lives within an hour's drive from me. I realize that so many of you do not have the immediacy of family. For me, the love of the grandchildren, Kevin, Gena, and Bridget became an incalculable healing force. I remember well a slogan I noticed in one of my doctor's offices: "If love doesn't heal it, *increase* the dosage." I only hope your family is the same emotional Rock of Gibraltar for you.

TIME IN GRADE

You can't depend on your eye if your imagination is out of focus.
—Mark Twain

If you served in the military, you can never forget the phrase "time in grade." From it flowed promotions and, best of all, the opportunity to get back to civilian life. Well, "time in grade," from another viewpoint, is something you may wish to ponder as you move forward in your role as a *widower* grandparent. The time you can devote to your grandchildren is ultra in their world. My late wife seemed more adjusted than I was to spending hours playing the repetitive and tedious games grandbabies love. The total number of times she willingly played Dinosaur Bingo must have set some sort of endurance record. How could you not love the triumphant face of my six-year-old when he was a winner? From the grandbabies' perspective, you are now doubling as both grandmother and grandfather. That's a tough act to pull off.

Most little ones have a very different understanding of death than we adults have. Small children don't seem to have grief as we know it. They quickly accommodate to "Mema" being in heaven, and their small world keeps turning. My Aidan (the six-year-old) sat next to me at my wife's funeral. As my eyes clouded over, little Aidan patted me on my shoulder and said quietly, "It will be OK, Papa." And from that moment, my little grandson became a player! Now I always try to be available to spin the wheel, roll the dice, and play the cards. Sometimes, when playing with the grandbabies seems like a chore, I try to recall Elizabeth's devotion, and I'm ready to roll.

Nobody has ever bet enough on a winning horse.
—Richard Sasuly

OH DEM BONES!

If at first you don't succeed, SKY DIVING is not for you!

Age is not a venerator of our bones and bodies. Some of you may be former big-time "jocks," guys that play scratch golf. In my case, from the earliest years, I lacked any hand-eye coordination. I was lucky to make the *debate* team, much less an athletic lineup. But for those of you who starred in athletics, please remember that trying to complete physically with an energy-loaded youngster is a risky game. Too many ERs are treating old-timers for broken hips and bones. We need to be very careful not to flex our "time experienced" (how's that for avoiding the word "old") bodies recalling the thrills of the deep passes, homers, and game—saving swishers of your youth.

What's more appropriate for our seasoned bones? Try this out for size—coach. Be a good and faithful *fan* on the sidelines, cheering on your grandchildren during their sports events. Yell your lungs out and have a great time doing it. And don't think for a moment that's only a boy's domain. Far from it. Girls too need a cheering Papa to praise their athletic skills. To make my day even more fun, I always bring along a folding chair, sunglasses, and plenty of water. You may well meet many other grandparents following the on-the-field exploits of their cherubs. After the final whistle has sounded, you, Granddaddy, can take over the role of *team trainer* and suggest a lunch of hot dogs for Daddy and your star player. It is a comfortable tab for you to pick up, and your grandson (or granddaughter) will be proud as a peacock that their Papa is watching and approving!

BEING A SUEH!

Being alone, fellow widower, is *not* an excuse for being a SUEH, an acronym for "showing up empty-handed." If you can't cook and you must travel some distance to attend a family gathering, try bringing some *nonperishable* items—tempting candies and cookies. If you are close by, hors d'oeuvres and inciting desserts can't miss. If none of the above are readily available, remember that flowers always soften all hearts.

Another hint to keep a high profile during family gatherings is what I term "gift hauling." Here's what I mean. FAO Schwarz or other kid's emporiums do *not* have a monopoly on gifts for kids. Try your local Dollar Store. Remember when you were a kid and adults gave you "a little something" just for you? It produced a world of thrills. Inside the Dollar Store (or an equivalent) is a fascinating collection of overstocked leftovers and odds and ends. Toy cars, dollies, books, crayons, caps—you will be amazed at what a dollar will buy. Even today, these are treasures little folks will cherish. A few minutes shopping there will give you a bundle of happiness to bring along on your next visit. So what if the stuff's shelf life is measured in minutes? The *idea* will have lots of longevity, and Papa will take a giant step in the minds of the little receivers. I tried this on Father's Day with my three. Bingo! I was the hit of the day. I'm already planning a trip to the Dollar Store for the Fourth of July stuff.

Here's another gift hint that worked for me. When you are asked to come to a birthday celebration of one of the grandbabies, bring along a few lesser gifts for the rest of the small ones. Little Aidan recently celebrated his sixth year in July at a fun-filled pirate's party. Besides my gifts for Aidan, I brought along two little bags of goodies for each of the twins. This bit of attention focused on them helped keep their wee "noses in joint." The twin's big day will come in January, reaching the ripe old age of three! Hopefully, I'll be there with big presents for the twins and some little ones for Aidan.

A thought on *receiving* gifts from your little ones, or big ones for that matter. Bill Cosby supposedly said, "The art of being a parent is making believe that getting 'soap on a rope' is the best present you ever received." This takes a bit of acting, but what a guideline to follow! As you open gifts on Father's Day, Grandparent's Day, or your birthday, sneak a peek at the faces of your grandbabies. Such anticipation for a good result! It's all part of the love that is the lubricant for happiness.

SPARE THE ROD

A quick thought on *discipline* as it relates to your grandchildren. Basic tenet, *you*, my fellow widower, are *out* of the kid business! Out! Yes, you have the combat medals and campaign ribbons (and cancelled checks) awarded for bravery in parenting. Now, as a granddaddy, try to sit back and enjoy the fruits of your labors. A case in point, when my son, Kevin, was a toddler, my parents showered him with love and understanding. But with the passage of time and aging, their attitudes changed.

My son tells me *now* that my own father (Rudy, God love him), later in his life, fell into an inconsiderate habit of trying to discipline him with a heavy dose of negativity. Sadly, teenager Kevin (in the mind of my dear and well-meaning father) was an overprivileged kid with little or no future. Maybe it was a sign of the times. The generational separation of a grandfather who struggled in the Great Depression and the sometimes "easy come, easy go" irreverence of today's affluent society. My father was a fine and upright man, a former schoolteacher, who found, late in life, success as an industrial filmmaker. Patience was not his middle name. When dealing with teenagers, Granddad was not at his best. Over time, a deep rift developed between grandfather and grandson, erasing any hope of a loving relationship.

From my son's birth, I have been very cognizant of creating a *loving bond* with him, often trying desperately to maintain it through those exasperating teen years. I remember my wife telling the then-teenager Kevin, "I love you but I don't like you!" Thank heavens, the teen years do pass. Or as my English friends say, "We prefer to send them to a boarding school until they are *done*!" Well, a part of getting them "done" is putting good stuff in and getting good stuff out, as the computer experts say. Now, as an emotionally needy widower, I thank the Lord every day for the loving closeness that has flourished over the years.

I was thrilled when Kevin asked me to be his best man at his wedding. Don't get me wrong. There's a few DNAs of my father's disciplinary quirks still lurking in me. When I was tempted to tell my six-year-old grandson, "Aidan, don't do that," my son subtly tells me that *he*, as Aidan's daddy, will handle the matter. It works in the eyes and minds of all of us. Oh, it is sometimes very difficult to *fermez la bouche*, but the payoff is another key development in *your* role as papa. And when your little ones rush to see you upon your arrival, maybe eager to discover what's in your traveling case, the verdict is in. Papa, you *are* truly something special!

HAVE A NICE TRIP?

In the first weeks and even months after your loved one has gone, you might feel a need for a change in your surroundings. A trip to "somewhere" might be just the ticket to provide a welcome relief. I'm not talking about visiting some friends or relatives or even children. No, what this section is about is *real* travel with a capital *T*. Some of you may already be experienced world travelers and others fall into that category of thinking of travel "someday," couples planning on taking trips together *after* retirement. Sadly, you are now alone. But does that rule out the value of a trip at this stage in your life? You may rightly say that taking a trip alone, without your beloved spouse, seems totally impossible. I know that I had the same feeling that a journey without my Elizabeth would not be possible. I have thumbed through dozens of travel folders, and now I'm ready to sally forth—alone!

Stop for a moment and realize the number of seniors in our nation today. Almost 10 percent of our population are sixty-five years old. And every day, it is estimated that over five thousand more folks light candles for that milestone birthday. And it is among these "gray hairs" that the "travel itch" is most prevalent. Scores of widowers just like us, at this very moment, are visiting exotic places, admiring new cultures, and are meeting new people. Why not! We certainly have the time, and hopefully, most of us have the funds to pack up and fly away!

The tourism industry long ago recognized this affluent senior market, and top-quality travel companies have specialized in satisfying the desires of senior singles and couples, developing exciting and exotic travel that does not tax the body and budget.

Elderhostel is perhaps the most popular (toll free 1-877-426-8056 or *www.elderhostel.*org). Overseas Adventure Travel is another (1-800-493-6824 or www.Oattravel.com). I suggest you click on Google with "senior travel" and see what comes up. I promise you, you'll be amazed at what's out there waiting for you to sign up.

Now let's assume you can visualize a vacation holiday without your love. I know it is difficult, but let's just look at a few factors that will come into play *if* you decide to give it a whirl. I'll call them my "commandments" for savvy travelers. I learned to apply each one the hard way after circumnavigating the globe twice and working in over fifty countries.

My *first commandment* for any serious travel is "Purchase travel insurance." Yes, it costs a few bucks, but it is worth the peace of mind it provides. Several times in recent years, health issues have forced me to cancel expensive cruises. *Without* travel insurance, I would have lost most of the sizable dollars I paid for the tickets. Insurance coverage not only covers tickets, it also covers unexpected health problems. Most policies will provide emergency air service for fast returns to your local hospital and immediate care at the nearest suitable hospital. You'll sleep better with this protection in your pocket. As the old phrase goes, "Don't leave home without it." InsureMyTrip.com allows you to compare over a hundred insurance plans. They can be reached toll free at 1-800-487-4722. Of course, your travel agent is also a contact to check.

My *second commandment* is "Be aware of health conditions in areas you'll visit."

If you're considering a trip *outside* the United States, please check with your doctor (or local government health officials) about immunizations you may need to protect yourself during your travels. When I visited China, I was required to have a yellow fever shot. After seeing some of the places on my itinerary, I appreciated the little bump on my forearm from the shot. So please don't take immunization lightly as "bugs" you haven't even dreamed about are lurking in strange places ready to harm you. I'm personally a top-rated coward when it comes to needles, but a sharp one in your doctor's office or a clinic before leaving can save you months of agony later. Maybe even your life! Of course, many advanced countries do not require vaccinations for visitors, so you might be able to sail or fly away needle free! Just be sure to check it all out before you close your suitcase.

My *third commandment is* "Create a traveling drugstore." Get with your doctor about your prescription needs. This is the information source you will need to create your own traveling medical "care package" containing all your prescription medicines and over-the-counter items. Count the days you'll be away and fill your package with the proper amount of drugs for each one. If you have tendency for sea—or airsickness, mention that to your doctor. Sleeping pills might also be discussed to battle jet lag. Bring along a *printed list* of your medicines with *both* brand and generic names as drug names vary in foreign locations. You may be able to purchase the same drugs in a foreign country, but the cost may be prohibitive and the source may be difficult to locate. On a ten-day cruise in the Caribbean, I ran out of my glaucoma drops. The ship's doctor gave me a note and prescription for a local drugstore on Grand Cayman. Yes, they had them at *twice* the price I paid in Clearwater! I was told I was fortunate the druggist even had a supply. So your traveling drugstore is very, very important whenever you start packing your bags.

My fourth traveling commandment is "Always carry your prescriptions," subject to the current "safety" restrictions. When traveling in our "prescription dependent" age, domestic or foreign, keep all of your prescription drugs in a *carry-on* bag.

This also includes contact lenses and cleaning fluids, even denture supplies. Customs and drug enforcement officials also recommend keeping your prescriptions in containers that show their origin and medical names. Carry-ons arrive *with you* at your destination. Lost or misplaced baggage can be a real trip spoiler. On our last major trip to Southeast Asia, my wife's major luggage case, containing all her dressy clothes, was "lost" by the airline for a week. Thankfully, she had her casual clothing in another case that *did* arrive with us. All our prescription drugs were also with us in our carry-ons. All carry-ons are now subject to current "safety" rules. Check with your airlines before leaving home.

And that brings us to my last but not the least *commandment* of travel, "Copy your important papers."

Years ago, on a trip to Greece I misplaced my passport (or it was stolen). Fortunately, I made a habit of *photocopying* each ID page of my passport, along with my airline tickets, medical information, travel itinerary, hotel reservations, and even copies of my traveler's checks. I also carried a spare set of passport-sized photos of my mug. When the missing passport issue came to light I was able to go to the American Embassy will all the proper identification. In a short time, I was issued a temporary ID, and the consulate started proceedings to issue a replacement passport. A day later someone anonymously slipped my passport into the embassy's night drop box. Never did find out the background of the so called "find". But having the "right stuff" to prove my identity was a relief in any event.

Back to the topic, please! After copying each document of importance *three* times, I put a set of the copies in 8 x 10 envelopes with my name and address on the outside. One set of copies I always keep in my carry-on. I put a set in two of our check-in bags. That way I'm covered three ways! A few cents spent at a copier store will make this protection a sure thing.

I won't go into any details of trip selections. As you are now a single person, the rates for accompanied land packages, cruises, and river trips may have a surcharge. I mentioned this in the section on finding suitable ladies to date. Keep asking your travel agent and hit the Google site frequently. There are always specials for singles popping up. My advice is *give it a go*, fellow widower! A change of scene will help some of the grief turn into happy memories.

SPIRITUALITY

> You changed my mourning into dancing;
> O lord, my God, forever will I give you thanks.
> —Psalm 30:13

I cannot write this book without a few thoughts on spirituality and the part it has played in shaping my grief and healing. As I mentioned before, healing to me started as a *sometimes* thing. I have conscientiously worked at transforming healing into a *more oftentimes* thing. The major energy to accomplish this was a foundation of faith I turned to during the most stressful of times in the struggle for healing. Please don't take this the wrong way. I am still of "little faith" far too often, taking too much for granted and unintentionally ignoring, stopping for just a moment, to offer thanks to our Maker for the splendid happenings of my life, past and present. The loss of my Elizabeth altered so many things, including my prayer habits.

Yes, I do pray every day but still give far too little of my time to this great exchange between our Maker and me. Yes, it is a "one-way call," and the answers may come so veiled we cannot even immediately recognize them.

Of course, you may be of a far different spiritual persuasion. Please, I am *not* a cheerleader for a particular church or faith. But dear fellow widower, don't you have moments where you wonder about the *soul* of your lost mate? Don't you "talk" with her, especially about major events that have unfolded in your life since her death? I know I do frequently, and it gives me solace. And this brings up the *perennial* question through all the ages of mankind: Is there *really* an afterlife?

Will we be joined with our departed wives again somewhere and forever? I have run these cogent thoughts by my fevered brain a thousand times.

Yes, my Catholic faith is founded on the teachings of Jesus that absolutely confirms a life ever after. "Whoever believes in me, even if he dies, will live" (John 11:25). All other major religions of the world have various versions of an afterlife as the centerpiece for their belief.

As I mentioned through the agony of my wife's final months and days, a dedicated Catholic priest, Father Gerard MacAulay adroitly and compassionately gave us needed spiritual support. Late at night, in the bleak waiting rooms of Palms of Pasadena Hospital, Father MacAulay was voluntarily there with our family and close friends. Quietly, he was a sentinel of hope everlasting. Hopefully, you had your own father or reverend or rabbi at your side. Perhaps a family member or close friend who offered prayers or just comforting words at the most anxious moments of your vigil. Faith in *any* form and the men and women who evangelize are the rocks we can depend on in times of massive dislocations in our lives. God love them and bless their unselfish work!

Recently, I ran across the following prayer written by a priest from the Marianist Mission in Dayton, Ohio. No matter what your faith or belief, this little prayer seems to hit the heart of our searching for answers!

Lord, thank You for another day
With this life of mine.
Give me the strength to live it well,
Whatever I may find.
Help me to use my hours wisely, for I cannot have them back.
Lord, thank You for another chance,
In which to try to be
A little more deserving

Of the gifts you've given me.
For yesterday is over,
And tomorrow's far away.
And I remain committed
To the good I do today!

HOW OTHERS SEE US

As we conclude our visits together, I thought you might be interested in some research I have dug up concerning widowers, remarriage, finances, health, etc. These are excerpts from several noted experts in the field and may have a broader meaning than my personal experiences. Take them for what they seem to be worth.

A survey by Bulcroft, Hatch, and Borgatta states that three out of a thousand women (age sixty-five and older) and seventeen out of a thousand older men remarry each year. The survey also stated that *remarriage provides the individuals with better health levels and improved financial status.* This is confirmed by another study by Smith, Zack, and Duncan stating that the death of a spouse causes a decline in the surveying spouse's health and economic status. Here's an important point in the survey: *Financial standing and health seems to be a major determiner in remarriage.*

A study of Canadians (aged fifty-five to sixty-five) stated that *men are more likely to remarry because social norms still look favorably on men marrying substantially younger women.* In contrast, older women who declined to marry are looked upon as liberated and autonomous.

One statistic of this Canadian study stated that following divorce, men are more likely to remarry in 3.4 years versus 3.6 years for women. The same numbers apply to widowers according to this study.

Next, a few thoughts from some world-renowned experts in the field of grief and healing. You may find them helpful and encouraging as you encounter the difficult days ahead. We will start with some ideas from the inquiring mind of Dr. Donald H. Kausler, author of *The Graying of America*. His research points that the *first stage* of grief for widows and widowers usually persists for thirty months, often longer. However, older men (rather than older women) will *repress* their emotional distress after the death of a spouse. This repression, the study concluded, may contribute to *earlier* deaths for widowers than widows.

Dr. Kausler's research team also compared the *life satisfaction* of older widowers and *non*widowers. Widowerhood, they reported, is *more depressing* for older men than for older women. Nevertheless, the study contained an encouraging thought. *Older widowers tend to possess greater self-confidence than they did before the death of their spouses.*

In an earlier chapter, I offered a few thoughts about selling your home and moving to a new location. Dr. Kausler's study concluded that *widowers are more likely to leave the house they shared with their late spouse than are widows*. And widowers are more than three times as likely to *relocate* to another state as widows are.

A recent *New York Times* story added a few dimensions to our widowerhood saga. "Men grieve differently than women," the *Times* stated. "They talk less—it's a rarity to find a man in a bereavement counseling session—and usually cry less in public."

Tom Golden, author of *Swallowed by a Snake*, wrote,

> Men spend more time around a gravesite, tending them as a sign of grief rather than talking or crying. People may not see it, so they assume men are not dealing with their grief, but they are in different ways.

Morton Kondracke, executive editor of *Roll Call* magazine and a Fox News contributor, wrote a book, *Saving Milly*, about his wife's fight against Parkinson's disease. In his book he stated,

> When she died, it was not totally unexpected because she had been sick for so long. But writing this book was my way of mourning, even before she died. I had no real companionship or real intimate relations. I had hoped to replicate my relationship. Milly and I were welded together—but I had no idea whether I could.

Mr. Kondracke was recently remarried twenty-two months after his first wife passed away. He said, "I consider myself very lucky to have been able to do it twice in the same lifetime."

In a recent Sunday edition of the *St. Petersburg Times*, book editor Margo Hammond wrote some very profound words.

> Grief is an island. The isolated kind in the middle of a vast ocean where ships and crew are marooned and all communication is cut off. When my mother died, I found myself feeling suddenly thrown off course. It was as if some navigational point, some star by which I had navigated my way through the world, had blinked off and I literally could not find my bearing.

Ms. Hammond recommended in her column several books that helped her through her grief. One best seller is *The Year of Magical Thinking* by Joan Didion. Another work suggested was *The Mourner's Dance* by Katherine Ashenburg. Of course, there are many other books you may wish to check out. A visit to your local library's information desk will help in your quest for excellent reading materials.

NOT THE BEGINNING OF THE END, BUT THE *END* OF THE BEGINING!

In the first agonizing months of World War II, the "odious apparatus of Hitler and his gang" (the words of Churchill) seemed invincible, winning victory after victory. It appeared this monstrous menace would soon have the entire world under its jackboot. Then a major battle loomed for control of Egypt and the vital lifeline of the Suez Canal. Defeat here would doom the free world. But it was not to be. The Allies were victorious! It was the start, the beginning of crushing the indescribable evils of Hitler. Following this resounding victory, Winston Churchill spoke to the British Parliament and the world using these inspiring words, "It is *not* the beginning of the end, it *is* the end of the beginning."

I chose these elegant words because I positively feel that this is also an "end of the beginning" for all widowers. *How* it happens and *when* it happens is the personal battle each of us must wage. I am now finally reaching the end of the beginning and am ready to move on.

With God's help, wonderful friends, and supporting family, you too can find that magical "end of the beginning" and move on! I hope you have progressed from being LOST, and have FOUND some of the ways to "recover." As we say adieu, I wish that one thought will always be your guide. **TODAY** IS THE *FIRST* DAY OF THE **REST** OF YOUR LIFE! MAKE THE MOST OF IT!

May the good Lord bless and keep you!

BOOK ENDORSEMENTS

Finally, a warm and witty, yet practical guide for the recently widowed man navigating the uncharted waters of loss, laundry, and lunches alone! The answers are all here in this "tool box".
Dr. Patricia Burkett PSY.D

I was left alone after a long and happy marriage. Your book "Lost & Found" (written by a widower for a widower) really tells WHAT we should do to handle grief, and sensible ways to get on with life. I unstintingly recommend this practical guide as a *must read* for any widower, young or old.
Frank P. Rock
Former special agent FBI,
Retired corporate security director.

Swanson's book "Lost & Found" became the foundation for a new approach for the ***Hospice of the Florida Suncoast*** to reach out to widowers during their first few months of being without their spouses. The vital topics in "Lost & Found" were developed into a series of ten seminars representing a completely fresh approach to help widowers in their most challenging times.

Printed in Great Britain
by Amazon.co.uk, Ltd.,
Marston Gate.